"Ain't Gonna Lay
My 'Ligion Down"
African American Religion in the South

Edited by
Alonzo Johnson
and
Paul Jersild

1996

University of South Carolina Press

Grateful acknowledgment is made to
the Lutheran Theological Southern Seminary and
the South Carolina Humanities Council
for their financial support of this project

Published in Columbia, South Carolina, by the
University of South Carolina Press

Manufactured in the United States of America

00 99 98 97 96 5 4 3 2 1

Library of Congress Cataloging-in-Publication Data

Ain't gonna lay my 'ligion down : African American religion in the
    South / edited by Alonzo Johnson, Paul Jersild.
        p.   cm.
    "This volume originates from 1993 conference sponsored by the
Center on Religion in the South . . ."—Pref.
    Includes bibliographical references.
    ISBN 1–57003–109–6
    1. Afro-Americans—Southern States—Religion.   2. Southern
States—Religious life and customs.   I. Johnson, Alonzo, 1957–   .
    II. Jersild, Paul T., 1931–   .
    BR563.N4A45   1996
    277.5′08′08996073—dc20   96–41291

Contents

Preface

This volume originates from a 1993 conference sponsored by the Center on Religion in the South, a program of the Lutheran Theological Southern Seminary in Columbia, South Carolina. The first two chapters are revised forms of lectures presented at the conference, while the subsequent chapters were solicited for this collection. Largely through sponsoring conferences and forums, the Center seeks to encourage the study and understanding of religion in the South. It is hoped that this purpose will be significantly furthered through the publication of this book.

The editors wish to express their thanks to Lutheran Theological Southern Seminary and to the South Carolina Humanities Council for providing financial assistance that has been instrumental to the publication of this volume.

Introduction

The subject material addressed in this volume reflects a growing interest in African American history and specifically in its religious expression. The religious life of the African American community is an important dimension of the larger history of religion in the South as well an important dimension of current southern religious expression. Before we turn to the specific areas addressed by the writers of this volume, we would like to make some general observations about religion as a phenomenon in the South. It is important to keep in mind that whatever level or dimension of religious life one is addressing—whether individual or corporate, worship or social activity, personal or congregational piety—one must not isolate the black religious experience from the rest of southern religion, for there is more interaction between them than has often been recognized. In fact, there has always been a symbiotic relationship between the development and structure of the religious life of African Americans and the religious life of non-African American southerners. Milton Sernett's *Black Religion and American Evangelicalism: The Protestant Missions and the Flowering of Negro Christianity, 1787–1865* (Metuchen, N.J.: Scarecrow Press, 1975) and Alfloyd Butler's fine Ph.D. dissertation, "The Blacks' Contribution of Elements of African Religion to Christianity: A Case Study of the Great Awakening in South Carolina" (Northwestern University, 1975), provide excellent examples of the cross-fertilization between African American and Euro-American traditions in the antebellum South.

Students of the South generally recognize today that if one is to know the South, one must know its religious life. This was not, however, always so. For many years the subject of religion in the South was generally left to denominational histories and did not play a noticeable role in the work of secular historians and sociologists. More often than not, religious expression in the South was the subject of mild curiosity or even ridicule, with attention focused on the more extreme aspects of folk religion among those who were uneducated and relatively isolated from the rest of society. One classic case of this is the common practice of referring to the snake-handling Pentecostal groups from Appalachia as key examples of southern piety rather than as the fringe groups that they are.

Today, as theologian and student of the South Samuel S. Hill has noted, professional observers of the South "can do no less than acknowledge the reality of religion and its formative influence."[1] He notes three factors that have helped account for this development and promoted an increase in the number of serious works addressing the role of religion: the visibility of religion and the emergence of religious studies as "a serious and maturing academic field"; the recognition that religion is an "integral factor" throughout much of the whole of southern life rather than a discrete subject that can be isolated from everything else; and finally the new image and status of the South, which have made all dimensions of southern life, including its religion, more respectable and important as a subject for study.[2]

At the personal level, anyone who has lived in the North and had occasion to move to the South is likely to be impressed with the impact of evangelical Christianity upon public consciousness and its influence on public life. While the spirit of secularism is evident in the South as well as elsewhere, the religious affirmation continues to be a notable feature of everyday life. This is apparent in many crass forms—messages in the electronic media, bumper stickers, and billboards—but it is also attested to by large numbers who make their way faithfully to Sunday and midweek worship. Southerners generally are more ready to assume the importance of religious belief at both the personal and the corporate level and are more likely to recognize and appreciate the integral role of the churches in maintaining the character of their culture. More often than not, this role is expressed in a conservative way in upholding values of the past that are important to the identity of the culture.

Within this larger socioreligious context, the authors who have contributed to this volume seek to understand the meaning of African American religious traditions. One of their tasks is to note the links that these religious traditions have to mainstream, southern, evangelical religion on the one hand and, on the other hand, to the "folk" traditions of African Americans living in the South. Moreover, there is a consistent effort in this volume to demonstrate the continuities between African American folk traditions and African traditions.

The discussions of African American "folk religious traditions" in this volume are not to be understood in the light of Joseph R. Washington's use of this phrase three decades ago in his *Black Religion*.[3] No book on black religion has caused more consternation among black theologians and scholars of religion. James H. Cone notes the publication of Washington's book as one of the principal factors behind the development of the black theology movement.[4] Black theologians were deeply disturbed by Washington's depiction of black religion as an expression of "folk" enclaves that were less than Christian. Black religion, he maintains, was folk religion because it was more focused upon matters related to racial survival than on the promotion of true Christianity. Washington describes folk religion as follows: "the spirit which binds Negroes in a way they are not bound to other Americans . . . it transcends all religious and socioeconomic barriers which separate Negroes from other Negroes."[5] As such, he claims, this folk religion is actually more concerned with racial interests than it is with the universal vision of the Christian faith. For this reason, Washington argues that black folk religion betrays the true, orthodox spirit of the Christian tradition. The problem with black folk religion is its reliance on conservative, white evangelical understandings of the New Testament. In a later book, Washington would alter radically his thesis and postulate that white Christianity was also a folk religion since it was complicit in the racial atrocities of American history and helped to create the staunchly hypocritical religious context in which black folk religion would thrive.[6]

As black theologians have done for more than twenty-five years, we, the editors and contributors, categorically disagree with Washington's thesis that there is not a true Christian vision among black Christians. We take issue with his view of black folk religion. While Washington is correct in pointing to the universal themes in the gospel, he does not give sufficient attention to the folk religious motifs which have always shaped Christian theological claims. All historical embodiments of religious faith bring with them the sweet scent of human life, struggles, aspirations, culture, beliefs, and, yes, folk traditions. It is impossible to get a true understanding of Western Christianity without grasping this fact. Folk religious expressions are not inherently xenophobic, racist, or narrow-minded, as Washington's treatment of black folk religion might imply. They can, in fact, be liberating and enormously powerful.

For the editors and authors of this volume, therefore, the idea and reality of black folk religion are not troublesome; nor are they to be regarded as deformations of true Christianity. Instead, the idea of a black folk religious tradition refers, in this work, to the peculiar ways in which African Americans "put flesh on their Christian beliefs." It refers to the religious practices, beliefs, customs, and traditions of African American Christians that are specifically rooted in their racial memories, their historical experiences, and their sociocultural heritage. These are the practices that make African American Christianity, alongside the other segments of the Christian community, what it distinctively is. Black folk religion, then, is that particular expression of faith emerging from a "conjuncture of

many streams—African, European, classic Judeo-Christian, and Amer-
indian,"[7] as all of these are meshed with folk culture of black Americans.
One who seeks to understand black folk religion must grasp its essential
connection to these other traditions in a world that has brought them all
together. Folk themes in black religion concern such practices and beliefs—described in this volume—as seekin' the Lord, ring shouting, dancing, pray's houses, ecstatic trances, spirit possession, singing folk, the use
of other music, tale-telling (Brer Rabbit tales, for example), and the like.
There are also the folk beliefs in phenomena such as hags, witches,
haunts, conjuring, sorcery, and so forth. These beliefs and practices form
the core of the alternative worldview that distinguishes the religious faith
of African Americans. They interpreted the Christian faith of whites and
converted it into their own unique possession. The title of this volume,
"Ain't Gonna Lay My 'Ligion Down" (taken from a spiritual), reflects this
religious heritage and its centrality to the African American ethnic identity.

One leading interpreter of African American history and culture in
South Carolina, Charles Joyner, upon observing the strong connection between black folk culture and black religion, commented that black slaves
"did not so much adapt to Christianity (at least not the selective Christianity evangelized to them by their masters) as adapt Christianity to themselves."[8] In the chapters of this volume the authors look at some of the
persons, customs, beliefs, and practices that demonstrate how African
Americans have adapted Christianity to themselves. The essays offer the
interpretation of scholars representing a wide range of humanities-
oriented religious scholarship. They reflect two principal foci: specific
themes and topics pertaining to black folk religion and the historical examination of the lives, ministries, and scholarship of persons representing
aspects of this folk heritage. Though the common thread that binds the
chapters is the subject of folk religion, there has been no attempt to force
a consensus among the authors as to their understanding of folk religion.
The methodological approach of all of the authors is principally phenome-
nological and descriptive rather than narrowly theological, though there
are clearly strong theological implications.

The opening essay is written by Alonzo Johnson, who is a systematic
theologian. Drawing on a wide range of well-known and lesser-known
historical and sociological works and important primary interviews, Johnson's essay examines the pray's house spirit and the seekin' the Lord
tradition in black southern religion. He proposes that the pray's houses
functioning in both past and present as an extension of the institutional
black churches provide the physical and conceptual context within which
to understand the heart and soul of black religion in the South. Pray's

houses are formal settings in many rural black communities that allow people in local areas to foster their own peculiar forms of spirituality and theology. The ritual and spiritual anchor of the pray's house spirit, Johnson says, is the African American practice of "seekin' the Lord," a distinctive type of conversion ritual. The unique fact here is the manner in which blacks have transformed the evangelical practice of seekin' the Lord into a rite of passage and part of their full-fledged cosmology. Johnson further contends that many historical, theological, and ethical analyses of slave religion fail in two key respects: they do not understand the true implications of the pray's house and seekin' traditions, nor do they comprehend how both of these traditions continue to shape black religion in the South today.

Jon Michael Spencer's thesis is that *rhythm* is the scarlet thread that conclusively maintains the continuity between African life and black life in the New World. Rhythm, for Spencer, has a supernatural quality that is symbolized in the mystical significance of the drum and drumming in African culture and further accented by African dance and ritual celebrations such as the ring shout. The rhythmic quality of the African soul is also seen in the spirituals, blues, dance, art, sermons, and lives of African Americans as well as those of other African descendants in the Americas. Spencer goes even further in suggesting that rhythm is the glue that holds together every facet of African American culture. Using the latest findings on black life from the disciplines of history, folklore, and ethnomusicology, Spencer asserts—echoing the singing group The Sounds of Blackness—that "the rhythm in our hearts is our freedom. . . . Will you give up your drum? No! Will you give up your rhythm? No!" Rhythm has set the black soul free and taught it to survive and to transcend the limits of its freedom.

William Courtland Johnson's essay focuses upon the question of morality in African American folk tales, namely the Brer Rabbit tales. This essay provides an excellent analysis of the varying ways in which the trickster figure, Brer Rabbit, is depicted in scholarly treatments of African American folklore. The most theoretical of the contributions to this volume, Johnson's essay notes the pattern in which academic studies of this topic have emerged over the years and provides insights into the reasons for their continuities and discontinuities. In addition to his broad analysis of the development of trickster scholarship, he proposes that the trickster figure gives us a fictional glimpse into the moral and spiritual center of African American life as it has faced brutality, triumph, and tragedy in this country.

The final essay with a folk religion theme draws specifically and primarily upon the experiences of African and African American women for the study of the concept of *motherwit*. Jacqueline D. Carr-Hamilton explores the symbolic and literary connections between African traditional transitions and the religious experiences of African American women. Her essay is punctuated as well with moving personal reflections. The concept of motherwit refers to the entire body of collective wisdom and spirit passed on from generation to generation by black women. Similar to Jon Michael Spencer's concept of rhythm, Carr-Hamilton's motherwit is a concept that defines the essence of the black female experience in the New World, as it had defined the experiences of the matriarchs in Africa. Motherwit is viewed as the key to the creativity and strength of black women. This study also explores the link between the idea of mother wisdom and the development of womanist theology, by far the most creative form of God-talk to emerge from the black theology movement in the past decade. Motherwit, she suggests, is in part a religious concept, but it is much more than this. It defines the essence of the folk culture of southern blacks, specifically in relationship to black women. Much attention in Carr-Hamilton's essay is given to the theological and literary reflections of womanist theologian Delores S. Williams and other black literary figures.

The last two essays are more historical in scope. Stephen W. Angell discusses the subject of folk religion by examining the work and contributions of three black Methodist preachers in the South Carolina Upcountry. Looking at the ministries, theologies, and practical experiences of Isaac (Counts) Cook, James Porter, and Henry McNeal Turner, Angell demonstrates how these ministers helped to contribute to their denominations and to the black religious tradition in general. He views these men as the cutting edge of a new generation of black religious leaders who could bring together the folk experiences of their people and the stringent sociopolitical demands forced upon them. These men were in the forefront in shaping the independent black religious tradition in the South, namely the African Methodist Episcopal Church, during the middle and latter decades of the nineteenth century. In this role they were also a part of the important shift of blacks from the Methodist Episcopal Church (North and South) to the newly formed black denominations.

The final essay, by Sandy D. Martin, is also historical in scope, examining the "ecclesiology and biblical interpretation" of James Walker Hood (1831–1918). During his very active ministerial career—he was a bishop for more than forty years and the senior bishop of his denomination for more than twenty years—Hood was one of the leading religious and civic leaders in the South. With a base in North Carolina, where he served as bishop of the African Methodist Episcopal Zion Church, Hood was in the forefront of the race movement of his era. Martin's essay accents Hood's role as a leader in the independent black churches of the South, well beyond the boundary of his own church, and pays special attention to the impact of Hood's religious vision in shaping his political perspectives.

Notes

1. Samuel S. Hill, ed., *Varieties of Southern Religious Experience* (Baton Rouge: Louisiana State University Press, 1988), 1.
2. Ibid., 1–2.
3. Joseph R. Washington, Jr., *Black Religion: The Negro and Christianity in the United States* (Boston: Beacon Press, 1964).
4. James H. Cone, *My Soul Looks Back* (Maryknoll, N.Y.: Orbis Books, 1984), 8.
5. Milton C. Sernett, *Afro-American Religious History: A Documentary Witness* (Durham, N.C.: Duke University Press, 1985), 50.
6. Joseph R. Washington, Jr., *The Politics of God* (Boston: Beacon Press, 1967).
7. Eugene Genovese, *Roll, Jordan, Roll: The World the Slaves Made* (New York: Vintage Books, 1976), 209.
8. Charles Joyner, *Down by the Riverside* (Urbana: University of Illinois Press, 1984), 141.

"Pray's House Spirit"

The Institutional Structure and Spiritual Core of an African American Folk Tradition

Alonzo Johnson

This essay examines the development, function, structure, and spiritual core of the pray's house spirit in African American religion. My thesis is that the pray's house spirit, both past and present, represents a central ethos of the religious life of African American southerners and a quasi-institutional setting within which to understand it. This is particularly true for Lowcountry South Carolinians, and the Gullahs, who will be the focus of this study.[1] The pray's house spirit—functioning as an extension of African American churches and communities—has provided a distinctive socioreligious context wherein folk beliefs and religious practices of African American southerners could prosper. The spiritual center of the pray's house spirit is the folk practice of seekin' the Lord. Thus this study will focus on two specific areas: the development of the pray's house spirit and the meaning of the practice of seekin' the Lord.[2]

My concern with the pray's house spirit emerges from strong personal and scholarly interests. To begin with, I am a product of the South Carolina Lowcountry, and as such I am very familiar with the folk beliefs and practices that have characterized our religious life for the past few centuries. My work also is directly related to the growing efforts among scholars to use the experiences, narratives, and traditions of African American slaves as bases for their constructive theological and ethical projects.[3] This study is distinguished from the others, however, by its use of many current stories and testimonies about seekin' the Lord, thus indicating the continuity between the spirituality of African American slaves and that of their descendants.

My use of the phrase "pray's house," as opposed to the more commonly used rendering "praise house," is based upon the conclusions drawn long ago in the studies of Samuel Lawton, whose research in the 1930s suggested that this was the interpretation of most Lowcountry

South Carolinians. He concluded that the name "pray's house" was derived from the socioreligious function of the institution. It was a place where one went to pray and to seek God. As one pray's house member on Saint Helena Island said, it was a place "way oner go fur pray." Thus the majority of locals who were interviewed by Samuel Lawton in his study of Gullah religious life referred to the places either as pray houses (without the possessive *s*), or as the pray-ers house, with an equal accent on the two syllables of the first word. Many Lowcountry persons, Lawton noted, freely changed verbs into nouns without adding the extra ending. One would hear them say, then, things such as "One pray, Den Annuder lead a pray'—Dat mak' two pray's." This practice remains true today for many Gullahs.[4]

De Place Way Oner Go fur Pray

As recently as two decades ago, pray's houses, or classrooms, as they are also called, were dotted all across the landscape of the Lowcountry of South Carolina and Georgia. Persons who came of age prior to the 1970s will remember how prevalent the pray's houses were in their communities. In some communities there was a pray's house in every area where blacks lived.[5] While the formal structure of the pray's house has all but disappeared from the black community, the pray's house spirit is very much alive. Reflecting a synthesis of beliefs from a variety of sources (African traditional religions and culture, American slaveocracy, Western Christianity, Western values) African American folk religion is reflected in such beliefs and practices as telling folk tales (Brer Rabbit and King Buzzard), conjuring, ring shouting, seekin' the Lord, hags, hants, ghosts, plate-eyes, drools and voodoo.[6] The folk religious traditions that I am concerned about clearly demonstrate the degree to which African American slaves were able to preserve much of their traditional African spiritual heritage while simultaneously meshing it with Western symbols and theological claims. In the folk religious traditions, we see clear evidence of the Africanization of American and Western Christianity.[7] The following description of the activities in one Johns Island pray's house communicates much about the socioreligious function of this central African American tradition of the American South:

They used to have prayer service in the house—only family then. Afterward, they began to have joint class [class meeting] from house to house. Then when we get the hall, we begin to have meeting there.

My daddy teach we how to sing, teach we how to shout, teach we how to go fast, teach we how to go slow. And then going to

meeting, or later going to church, he'll teach we how to behave yourself when we get out to different places before we leave home.[8]

This description of the activities in the Moving Star Hall pray's house of
Johns Island (which, incidentally, was not established until 1914) is true
to the function that these institutions have fulfilled in the South Carolina
Lowcountry for more than a century.

The function and structure of the pray's house spirit—if not its actual
historical emergence—can best be understood in light of the development
of two distinct traditions within the African American South, namely
"brush arbors" and the plantation missions. It was in the context of their
brush arbor meetings on plantations that slaves first began to forge from
the crucible of their African experience and the terrors of their inservitude
a vision of Christianity that would be distinctively their own. In the night,
out of sight and hearing of the big house, the brush arbors were the sacred
spaces, the holy ground upon which slaves stood as they sang, prayed,
shouted, testified, preached, planned their escape, and otherwise did what
they felt spiritually led to do. The key to the brush arbor tradition was its
relative secrecy and its being in the control of the slaves themselves.[9]

When the attitudes of southern planters concerning the Christianization of their slaves changed, more opportunities appeared for evangelizing
and providing religious instruction for slaves. In many instances, masters
would allow the senior slaves in the quarters to use their cabins as places
for religious meetings. The spirituality that was forged in the brush arbors,
coupled with the folk traditions that were forged in the religious meetings
in the slave quarters, provided the impetus for the formation of the pray's
house spirit and later the independent black churches in the South Carolina Lowcountry.[10]

Another major factor in the development of the pray's house tradition
is the growth of the Plantation Mission System (PMS), the institutional
embodiment of white evangelical efforts to introduce Christianity to
southern slaves en masse. After the 1820s, on the heels of the Vesey and
Turner insurrections, there was a concerted effort on the part of white
denominations to take the Gospel to the plantations, where the slaves
were.[11] Many plantation owners and southern church leaders began to see
Christianization as the only means of "civilizing" and controlling their
slaves. Thus groups like the Methodist Episcopal Church spent more than
a million dollars in such efforts. (As early as 1809 the Methodist Episcopal
Church had appointed individuals such as the Reverend James H. Mallard
to begin a concerted effort to convert blacks in the South Carolina Lowcountry, and by 1829 William Capers had been appointed full time to this
task.)[12]

The Pray's House Spirit and the Institutional Black Church

In the postbellum period, the pray's houses in the South Carolina Lowcountry maintained some of the functions of the PMS, particularly that of helping to localize evangelism and fellowship activities within particular communities and on plantations. Guthrie, for example, notes that on the antebellum and postbellum plantations of South Carolina, all of the local denominations had their own pray's houses, where their slaves and freedpersons could go for praying, teaching, singing, testifying, and preaching.[13] Moreover, Methodists and Baptists, more than any other groups, were also effective in utilizing the leadership skills and influence of respected men and women on the plantations in helping to spread their message and to convert other slaves, as noted above. Often they would allow the slaves to establish their own patterns of worship, preaching, singing, and other religious activities under the leadership of these respected spiritual figures in the plantation community. This raises two perennial issues for our consideration. First, it underscores the fact that there was a very strong connection between the existence of pray's houses and the spread of Christianity among slaves. It would be naive at best and egregious at worst to suggest that these were truly independent institutions in an absolute sense. Nonetheless, it is true that they did indeed help to provide the institutional space for the growth of the leadership patterns and style of spirituality that emerged in the pray's houses. White denominational leaders and missionaries often noted, to their dismay, how much influence the slave "elders" and "mothers" had upon the religious beliefs of fellow slaves.[14] As one such person stated:

We have had some trouble at another place, occasioned by the puffing up of Father S., as he is called, but plantation authority forbids his guiding the people. They have appeared spellbound, not to move or think without him. He a poor creature of dust imagines himself to be the Great Shepherd whose voice alone "the sheep know," and whom alone the true sheep will follow. . . . We visit the plantations and explain as far as possible. God grant us brighter days and better times.[15]

The authority that is attributed to this particular plantation preacher reflected the type of reverence that slaves, and later many free blacks, had toward their spiritual leaders, whose place of prestige and power cannot be understood without some reference to the institutional setting that we have described here as the pray's house tradition.

Among South Carolina Sea Islanders, the pray's house was the place where persons who were seeking to join the Church or to become Christians would go to be instructed in the principles of the Christian faith. And when one was baptized, the pray's house was the first place where one went to formally become a part of the church and community. One current resident of Wadmalaw Island, South Carolina, says the following about the pray's houses that she attended as a youngster on the island:

> And that Sunday night then they had to take me over into the Prayer House. I still couldn't, although I was baptized, go and sit on the front seat. Until these leaders, and one of the older sisters of the meeting house, come back there and git me and lead me on by my arms from the back bench to the front seat. Then I became a Christian. Now you go in church, you don't know who is a Christian from not a Christian. But at that time if you are not a Christian you had to sit on the back bench. You couldn't mix with the Christian people.[16]

She goes on to say, in describing the relationship between the pray's houses and the churches:

> The church is the headquarters. You know the meeting house is . . . where you get your training to go on into the church. Tuesday, Thursday and Sunday nights. That's when you go to meeting. Those three nights were reserved strictly for meeting. On Tuesday night, that's when you testify. The mans git up to the desk and they talk from the Bible, tell us what they know about the Bible from the Bible teaching. Helping us on the way on to God. And then on Thursday night you have experience from the women, they sing a song and then they testify what God had done for you, how he bring you from a mighty long way. They just testify and keep on talking 'bout the Lord. Then on Sunday night then the man preaches. They get up to the desk and open the Bible and they take a text from the Bible like the 11 chapter of Hebrews or 15 chapter of John. What ever they want to talk about. And we sit and I listen and clap.[17]

From this excerpt and similar references, I will summarize the relationship between the churches and the pray's houses in South Carolina. To begin with, we note that they provided the necessary space within which denominations could break down their congregations into smaller units (Methodist classes and Baptist societies, for example) and thereby create more intimacy among members. Moreover, the pray's houses gave the churches a context wherein they could examine their members, new converts, and candidates for membership. In fact, Maggie Russell's testimony seems to suggest that one did not appeal directly to the church for membership; one first went to the pray's house. And it was there where, having been escorted from the rear to the front seat, one could now participate and "mix with the Christian people." Lawton stresses this point more fully when he posits that "the Pray's House definitely assists the church in the examination of candidates for church membership."[18] It was in the pray's house that new seekers had to make the first public statement about their visions or dreams or, to put it differently, conversion experiences. And in this context, where they were judged by family members, friends, and others from the community—people who knew them best—candidates had to convince others that they had really been converted: "One hafter show a good experience of de Pray's house or dey'll turn you down and make you seek mo!"[19] After successfully completing this examination, candidates were allowed to remove their white seekin' clothes and formally join the church.

The pray's houses also supported the churches by encouraging their weaker members and strengthening their faith through prayer, fellowship, and instruction. This "moral influence" helped to bring the spiritual voice and vision of the church directly into the neighborhood and indeed into the homes of believers, thus curbing or at least forestalling potentially destructive behavior patterns among its members. This latter point is particularly important because it gives us a sense of the overall social impact of the pray's house tradition in southern communities. Patricia Guthrie, for example, notes that the pray's houses helped to enforce the informal plantation system of just and unjust laws, which governed the behavior of persons within this context. Plantation elders and leaders judged the morals of their members, and when a member was found to be in conflict with communal standards, that individual was brought to trial. The judge and jury in this case were members of the pray's houses, and the system of jurisprudence to which they appealed consisted of their own laws, which they describe as "just laws." Persons who went outside this informal system to adjudicate their cases before white authorities were said to participate in a system of "unjust laws" and would thereby subject themselves to being ostracized by their communities. Thus there was a de facto judicial system in communities like Saint Helena that was undergirded by the informal structure of the pray's houses.[20]

The Pray's House Spirit: An African American Rite of Passage

Nowhere is the socioreligious function of the pray's house spirit more clearly demonstrated than in its role in socializing children. Thus my reference to the significance of pray's house rites of passage.[21] Among African-American slaves and their descendants in the American South, the pray's house spirit provided the ritual framework within which children could pass from childhood into adulthood. Children generally joined the church and pray's house around the age of twelve, the age of accountability. The pray's house spirit and the churches were the first formal institutions, outside of the family, into which young people were socialized. Thus when a child reached the age at which she or he could join the church or the pray's house, it was a significant moment. Seekin' was one aspect of a process that Guthrie has described as "catching sense," which, "broadly speaking, represents that time in a child's life when he/she is said to learn right from wrong and good from evil. It is also the time when children start to understand and remember the meaning of social relationships." She notes that this process begins as early as the age of two and climaxes when the child reaches the age of twelve or so. The relationships that she refers to here are principally those that are established with family and neighbors as the individual who is catching sense accepts the communal norms that have been passed on. To catch sense is to become an adult, a responsible person, a full human being. Catching sense entitles the individual to participate fully in all of the religiosocial traditions of his or her community.[22] Pray's house and church membership, therefore, had a strong social component, helping to bring children into adulthood.[23]

Gender and Authority in the Pray's House Tradition

Questions regarding gender roles and structures of authority were also critical in the pray's house spirit. I will look briefly at the question of gender roles in the pray's houses before moving to the second half of this study. Mrs. Maggie Russell's description of her pray's house experience is helpful on this point. According to her, the pray's houses of Wadmalaw Island met three times weekly: Tuesday, Thursday, and Sunday evenings. On Sunday evenings, the "seekin' mothers" escorted the new members to the front of the meeting room, where they would be welcomed into the inner circle of the pray's house. On Tuesday evenings the men were in charge of activities, including leading the singing and praying. On Thursdays the women were in charge of the services, leading the singing, testifying, and praying. A similar pattern of activities was noted by Guthrie and Lawton in their earlier studies of pray's house traditions. The structure of the Saint Helena Island pray's houses that Guthrie observes was as follows: A leader, always a male; a committee of four persons, males and females; a deacon, who functioned as an overseer; and the general membership, consisting of both males and females. Women were intricately involved in these groups, but they were not leaders, just as they were very active in their local churches but not as pastors. In other studies of Lowcountry pray's houses, however, women did function as leaders. Lawton, for example, cites evidence of female leadership in pray's houses as far back as the 1930s.[25] This is a significant fact, given what we know about the influence that pray's house leaders had upon their communities at large. Pray's house leaders were regarded as the wisest and most spiritual people of their communities. They were leaders in all phases of local communal life. The fact that women could serve as leaders in such settings says much about the significance of their contributions to particular southern communities.[26]

One other aspect of the subject of gender and authority in the pray's house tradition is the degree to which pray's houses were in the complete control of laypersons, not clerics. This was true for those in Baptist as well as Methodist churches. Given the significance of pray's houses as an extension of local congregations into certain remote areas, this is no accident. In rural Baptist and Methodist churches there is and always has been a shortage of ordained clergy. It is very common for ministers to pastor several churches simultaneously and for congregations to meet only twice a month for worship.[27] There were sometimes, in fact, rifts between the work of the church and the activities of the pray's houses. In my conversations with oral historian Vennie Deas-Moore, for example, she noted that the AME ministers in the 1920s and beyond in some Lowcountry South Carolina communities discouraged members from participating in the pray's houses because it was a threat to their power and authority over their members.[28] Moreover, it is also true that when ministers did become active in the pray's houses, they were required to have the same type of religious experiences, dreams, visions, and testimonies as their parishioners.[29]

The existence of female prayer bands, or prayer circles, represents another aspect of female leadership within southern communities, pray's houses, and churches. While I have not been able to trace their origins directly back to the pray's houses, it is clear from my research that their function is based solidly upon the socioreligious foundations that were laid in the pray's houses. To this day these groups, composed primarily of women from local communities and churches, continue to function. They are under the control of no particular denomination, though they represent the dominant group in a given community. The primary function of the groups is spiritual in that they go around at appointed times to visit and pray for the sick in their communities and to care for families in which heads of households have died or become ineffective. So at given times these women use their domestic skills in caring for children, cooking, cleaning, nurturing, and so on; but they are always praying for the needs of individuals and families. These praying women also use their time in people's homes to teach and study the Bible.[30] This seems to me an important fact because it indicates further how African American southern women, particularly South Carolinians, find ways—within and outside of the organized churches—to exercise their leadership and perfect their gifts.

"When You Seek and Get Your Religion": An African American Conversion Ritual

If the pray's house provided the quasi-institutional structure for the development of African American religious traditions in the South, the practice of seekin' the Lord was the spiritual foundation upon which this institution was established. In essence, the seekin' experience in African American folk religion is a conversion ritual. It is through the experience of seekin' the Lord that individual believers are ushered into the inner circle of the socioreligious worldview of their community. Thus seekin' the Lord is at the same time the most intensely private and one of the most communally controlled rituals in African American folk religion.

Margaret Washington Creel has argued that seekin' (as a Christian ritual experience) was formally introduced to African American slaves by white Methodist missionaries. In evangelical worship services, slaves learned the importance of making public confessions of faith. They were encouraged to come up to the altar of the church to "receive Christ in their lives." Seekin' was for them the means whereby they gained entrance into the life of the church. Evangelical revivalists such as Charles Grandison Finney—the great Congregationist revival preacher of the last century—developed certain "new measures" to encourage sinners to come forward in the church and seek the Lord. One such practice was the use of the "anxious bench," a place in the church where persons who wanted to receive Jesus into their lives would gather, pray, and wait for their lives to be changed.[31] In evangelical Protestantism, then, seekin' the Lord was in essence a central component of the conversion ritual. The practice of seekin' the Lord in the evangelical tradition represented one aspect of the radical democratization of the faith, with all persons, irrespective of race, class, or creed, expected to publicly affirm their faith in Jesus.[32]

For white evangelicals seekin' the Lord centered around the dramatic moment of the conversion experience. This was most often induced in a formal worship service or some similar context such as a prayer meeting or protracted revival meeting. While there were exceptions, the core elements of this process centered on what took place at the meeting.[33] Finney explains: "The first that I ever heard of under that name [anxious meetings] were in New England, where they were appointed for the purpose of holding personal conversation with anxious sinners, and to adapt instruction to the cases of individuals, so as to lead them immediately to Christ."[34]

The challenge before us is to see how his particular model of seekin' the Lord and the ritual experiences emerging from it functioned within the socioreligious context of the African American pray's house tradition. Within the folk religious traditions of the African American South, seekin' was transformed from a mere conversion ritual into the fundamental component of the African American worldview. It became a rite of passage, a means for the socialization of children and adults into the sociopolitical life of their communities. Moreover, it was the major spiritual requirement for membership in the churches and pray's houses. As a rite of passage, the seekin' experience is similar to African initiation rites, wherein adolescents are initiated into adulthood. In each context, the initiation process entails both spiritual and social meaning for the community. African American slaves transformed the evangelical seekin' experience into an initiation rite, with a strong sense of their African socioreligious heritage. Like certain areas of African American life, the seekin' experiences that we will discuss here embody what W. E. B. DuBois so eloquently described as the eternal "twoness" within the "Souls of Black folks."[35]

Much of what is known about the seekin' patterns in black southern religion is taken from the conversion narratives, personal stories, and testimonies of former African American slaves and their descendants as well as the numerous former-slave narratives collected under the umbrella of the Works Progress Administration. Other resources include the Lawton dissertation, cited earlier in this essay, which was done during the same period as the WPA interviews, and *God Struck Me Dead*, a collection of narratives based on the experiences of Tennessee former slaves, which is perhaps the most famous of the religious narratives.[36] Finally, I include many current conversion narratives, thus examining the continuity between present and past African American seekin' practices.[37]

Observers of the religious situation on antebellum plantations readily noticed how evangelical revivals helped to influence the religious situations on the plantations. Central to this development was the seasonal rise in the number of children and adults who were actively seekin' the Lord. As Elizabeth Browne, an observer of the plantation life of slaves on Hilton Head Island, South Carolina, notes:

In the winter most of the children were "seeking and praying." The older people said. "They do hang their heads and pray"; and they were not allowed to do much of anything else for fear they would "be turned back" [backslide from their Christian commitment]. . . .

These religious revivals were a source of much disturbance in school routine. . . . We cannot call these "religious excitement"; the young seekers were in a stupid and lethargic condition. Some children were not allowed to come to school for fear they would be turned back.[38]

These revivals helped to create the atmosphere wherein the pray's house ritual of seekin' the Lord could thrive. In the connection between the spread of revivals on the plantations and the rise in interest in seekin' the Lord, we see further evidence of the symbiotic relationship between the institutional churches of the South Carolina Lowcountry and the pray's houses that I have described thus far. If not from the pray's houses, individual children and adults certainly felt pressure from their churches and communities to begin seekin' the Lord at a young age, usually around twelve.[39] It was not unusual, however, to have individuals beginning to seek as early as the age of eight. As one participant said, "The Lord started me out when I was eight years old. We tried to seek the Lord. I went out on Saturday evening behind a stump."[40] Publicly seekin' the Lord was an act of great social significance in terms of becoming a part of the adult world of church membership, pray's house membership, and the assumption of adult responsibilities. One who had successfully "sought" the Lord was supposed to come out of this experience with a new sense of spiritual and ethical responsibility and mission. So there was indeed pressure upon young people to engage in the ritual of seekin'. One young seeker described his experience thus: "My first experience came one night just after I had gone to bed. I was twelve years old at the time, and it had never occurred to me that I had to *die* [emphasis mine]. . . . I was not asleep but had just closed my eyes when I saw, in a vision, a beautiful little white chariot floating through the air; and I was in it."[41] Although this particular seeker was moved to begin the process at the age of twelve, his climactic experience did not come until he reached his eighteenth birthday. At that point he actually "came through" and saw his vision, during which the Lord said to him, " 'My little one, thy faith hath made thee whole. Amen.' I shouted for joy."[42] Children were strongly encouraged to seek the Lord because it was their means of joining the church. Those who had passed the age of accountability without having done so were reminded of their need to "get religion." One eloquent Tennessee-born former slave put it this way:

After I was fifteen they told me that I should get religion. I asked what that was, and they scolded me so greatly that I decided to try and get one. I thought one time that I had got religion, but I had not seen anything especial to convince them that I had been converted. I then prayed again and again but failed, that year, to get religion. When the next revival started I began at once to seek religion, and I found the Lord precious to my soul.[43]

The persons who scolded her for not having "gotten her religion," we would be safe in assuming, were not strangers to her. They were family members, church and pray's house leaders, and people who otherwise were aware of her condition. We note also that she linked the time of seekin' directly to seasonal revivals. She began to seek the Lord as a result of the influence they had upon her life. Lawton notes that it was not uncommon for students to be excused from school while they were seekin' the Lord because going to school might have turned the seeker back to his or her old life of sin.[44]

At any rate, the difference between an individual who had found the Lord and one who had not was the key difference between one who was a "church member" and one who was a "real Christian." In an oral interview with Vennie Deas-Moore, Louise White put it this way:

LW: You join the church . . . as a member. You're a member of that church and when you get to be a Christian, then you join back as a Christian of the Church, and when you first join, you join as a member; you're not Christian yet. And you join when you get a Christian [sic], you go back in there for a Christian.

VD-M: Do you seek both times?

LW: No! No!

VD-M: When do you seek?

LW: Say like you go in church now, and you just join the church as a member. When you seek and get your religion, see you go back, they put you as a full member of the church [emphasis mine].

VD-M: When you seek, you're a full member?

LW: Full member.[45]

Whereas anyone in the community could join the church, only "proven" seekers could become full members. Full members were individuals who could participate in all of the sacred rituals, including baptism, the Lord's Supper, and singing in the choir.

Thus we accent the significance of the seekin' experience as a rite of passage into the socioreligious core of African American life in southern communities. In discussing the significance of seekin' the Lord as an initiation rite, we recall Victor Turner's statements about such rites. He argues that they involve three stages, the goal of which is to produce a new individual. Those stages are separation of initiates from their social group (the experience of "death"); the experience of marginality, a state in which individuals are stripped of their former identity and prepared for a new one; and finally, the return to the community as a regenerated, whole person, fully capable of participating in every aspect of communal life.[46] In examining the development and the stages in the seekin' process we see these three phases clearly and distinctly. "Getting religion" was at one and the same time a very public experience and an intensely private one. As a private experience, it prepared the seeker for a religious epiphany that was to be every bit as revelatory and spiritually transformative as Moses' burning-bush experience in the Hebrew tradition. As a communal ritual, seekin' the Lord successfully prepared children for two ceremonies that were central to the African American life in southern communities: the welcoming ceremony in the pray's house and the baptismal experience in the church. This latter experience was particularly significant for persons who were baptized as Baptists, a church in which the tradition of baptism is so strong.

Persons who "came through" were invited to be baptized in the church. Maggie Russell, a vibrant South Carolinian from Wadmalaw Island, says, in describing her conversion experience, that Jesus told her to "go tell Peter Singleton to baptize you. Tell your Pastor to baptize you, in the Name of the Father, Son, and the Holy Ghost. And he say everything will be allright."[47] The significance of the public baptism is beautifully accented in Howard Thurman's reflections on his experience as a young initiate into the life of his Baptist church in Daytona, Florida.

> I was baptized in the Halifax River. On Sunday morning everybody met at the church after Sunday School. We did not hold the morning service in the church. Instead, a procession was formed outside. The candidates for baptism, in white robes, were led by the minister and the deacons, who were dressed in black waterproof clothing. . . . This procession moved down the middle of the street.

An individual led the group in singing:

Oh, mourner, don't you want to go,
Oh, mourner, don't you want to go,
Oh, mourner, don't you want to go,
Let's go down to Jordan, Hallelujah.

Then the crowd picked it up:

Let's go down to Jordan,
Let's go down to Jordan,
Let's go down to Jordan,
Hallelujah.[48]

While Thurman does not connect his experience to a seekin' process as such, the language of the song ("mourner," and "go down to Jordan") is the language of the seekin' tradition in its most pristine form. The water imagery, the act of journeying across or going through water, was a metaphor for having "come through" the great period of personal struggle and growth. Nothing was more significant than water in explaining the visionary component of seekin'.[49]

The welcoming services in the pray's houses went hand in hand with the joy and celebration of the baptismal celebration. The young seeker was not only introduced to the life of the church but also exposed to the inner world of the pray's house tradition. As Maggie Russell explained, the pray's house is where seekers on Wadmalaw Island went to have their experiences authenticated. We have noted earlier that, in her description of pray's house tradition that she experienced in South Carolina, Russell emphasized the fact that the new members of the pray's houses were separated from the older members until they had been ushered to the front of the fellowship circle.[50] And as she described this experience, Russell clapped her hands, sang, and imitated the joyous celebrations that were seen as the goal of the pray's house service. Russell's Wadmalaw Island pray's house was a place for teaching, fellowship, and nurturing, a place where young people could be trained under the influence of older persons. This was a communal experience, an act of empowerment, a spiritual birthing rite.[51]

This brings us to the second stage of the seekin' process, the period of withdrawal. In all of the narratives and testimonies that we have examined, the seekers described having to go through a period of withdrawal wherein they were excused from normal daily activities to spend time in prayer, fasting, and otherwise seekin' the Lord. This withdrawal stage could last as long as three months, but the usual period was about two weeks. The withdrawal experience was an intensely private one, for it was when the individual prepared for the journey into the Kingdom of God. The withdrawal motif is indicative both of the process and of the places to which people retreated as they were seekin' the Lord.[52] This is perhaps, as I have suggested above, one of the more paradoxical elements of the seekin' tradition.

The slave spirituals communicated the loneliness of the withdrawal experience. With passion they sang, "I couldn't hear nobody pray, I couldn't hear nobody pray, way down yonder by myself, I couldn't hear nobody pray." Being "down yonder by myself" was the nadir of a journey that another spiritual depicts as "going down that lonesome road." It was a categorically private affair because only the individual could wrestle with the Almighty. It was appropriately regarded as a time of death. This withdrawal, wilderness motif also has a communal element, however. Dying represented the cessation of old ways and ideas, a denial of self in order to be awakened to God's laws and to the moral and spiritual expectations of the church, pray's house, and community. Moreover, in dying to the old ways of life, an individual was signifying readiness to accept the moral discipline and spiritual wisdom of the pray's house and church. The seeker indeed understood that "true religion" was neither inherited from one's parents nor passed on simply by participation in the ritual act of baptism; rather, one had to "seek" in order to "get religion."

Again Maggie Russell helps in underscoring both the nature and the meaning of withdrawal. As she notes:

> This is a story, a true story. You had to go out in the night in the dark, you know when first dark comes in. You go out there and you bow down under a oak tree. I could look at the top a dat tree, see [as she points off into the direction of a distant tree] dat skinny oak tree, dats the tree I prayed under, when I was a little girl. That's where I seek my religion. And 12:00 o'clock at night, 11:30 P.M., somebody a wake ya up: "Maggie, Maggie!" And I wake up. And I say, "O I Know what that is, time for me to go out." It was time for ya to go out.[53]

Russell's key references here are to the place where she did her seekin', under the tree, and to having set aside a specific time for doing it. For others the context for seekin' the Lord, and the place where the vision came, was the graveyard, near a body of water, in the woods, and in the church, among others. The graveyard theme is seen in the following excerpt from a former slave:

> When I was converted I had gone about five days without eating, and I was in a graveyard by the side of my grandfather's tomb. There

I heard a voice saying, "Rise, Mary." At first I decided not to rise, but then I heard the voice again and all at once from a very cloudy sky came a beautiful sun. Then I jumped up and shouted to the Lord and started singing: "Give me that good old-time religion."[54]

The large number of references to the outdoors as the place where persons went to do their seekin' underscores why this experience is often referred to as a wilderness experience. The wilderness was symbolic of the entire stage of withdrawal in the seekin' process, symbolic of both the nature of the seekin' experience and the place where it happened. Thus seekers sang:

> Tell me how did you feel when you come out the
> wilderness, come out
> the wilderness, come out the wilderness,
>
> Tell me how did you feel when you come out the
> wilderness, come out
> the wilderness, come out the wilderness,
>
> Leaning on the Lord.
>
> I felt like shouting when I come out the wilderness,
> felt like shouting when I
> come out the wilderness,
>
> Leaning on the Lord.

And they sang:

> If you want to find Jesus,
> go in the wilderness,
> Go in the wilderness, go in the wilderness,
> Mourning brudder, go in de wilderness.[55]

When asked to locate the place where the wilderness was, one former slave put it this way: "Anywhere outdoors away from folks dey calls de wilderness." Others saw the wilderness as "de old fields and pine woods round my house."[56] The places where people went to seek the Lord varied, but the wilderness motif remained constant. Moreover, we should note that, generally speaking, persons were not actually required to leave their homes while they were seekin'. The seekers went out at designated times.

"I Too Sorry for My Sins"

The dominance of the withdrawal motif in the seekin' experience also underscores the next important issue: Why did individuals begin to seek the Lord? The intensity and sincerity that seekers express during their time of seekin' is graphically indicated by the fact that the seekin' process is so intense and demanding. Seekers fasted and prayed very earnestly during their time of seekin'. As one aged seeker says, "Can't tell me wunner can pray with de belly full." The act of fasting was also, however, an expression of contrition, or remorse over one's spiritual plight. "I didn't eat much when I bin prayin'. I too sorry for my sins and too full of religion."[57] Seekin' and finding the Lord are more important than food.

At any rate, two reasons stand out as primary motivations for people to seek the Lord. The first were communal mandates and pressures. It was expected; at times it was demanded. The implications of this expectation were recognized by everyone concerned. The words of one seeker put it best:

> When I was twelve years old I wanted to join church. My father told me that I had better not come home unless I seen something [had a vision]. When I joined I just didn't see anything, and I was scared to go home, but just as I stepped out the door the heavens opened up, and I seed angels flying around. I ran to my father then.[58]

At the appropriate age, people were expected to begin seekin' the Lord, accepting the socioreligious demands of their community by doing what was expected. The journey toward God was taken by many as a matter of course.

In addition to the influence of communal expectations, individuals were frequently prompted to seek the Lord because of their personal experiences with grief and sickness, the latter defined in this instance in the most general sense as feelings of emotional, physical, and spiritual distress. The narratives and testimonies demonstrate the very African-centered notion that all illnesses have a spiritual point of origin. Thus sickness, they believe, is a result and a sign of sin, either voluntary or involuntary. So persons who were unconverted took sickness as their sign to get right with God. As one individual noted, "When I was about twenty-two years old I got sick, and I remember that then I began to feel bad because of the life I was leading. I thought about the Lord and began to pray to him for forgiveness of my sins."[59] He went on to describe the incident in more detail:

One day, after I had taken a lot of medicine and had about everything the doctors could give me, I remember lying on my back looking up at the ceiling. Of a sudden I saw beyond the ceiling and
seemed to see the heavens open and a hand come forth which hit
me in my face, while a voice said to me as loud as thunder, "I am a
doctor." That very minute I seemed to get stronger. I got well a
little later.[60]

In these narratives, illnesses often returned when persons relapsed to their
sinful ways. As one seeker confessed: "A long time after the first spell I
got sick again . . . I prayed and told God how I had not done what I had
promised. [And a few days later] . . . immediately I gained strength, and
in less than five minutes I felt strong enough to get up."[61] The frequency
of the references that link seekin' with the experience of personal sickness, whether it is physical, emotional, or spiritual, accent my point about
the individualistic/communal dialectic in the seekin' the Lord tradition.[62]

The Moral Mandate

The moral theme in the seekin' experience further accents both the
communal and individualistic impulse in the pray's house spirit. Successfully seekin' the Lord always entailed more than a personal experience
with God; one had to live in obedience to known communal norms. Persons who lapsed into old habits or otherwise did not obey accepted cove-
nants were ridiculed for such behavior. One former slave, questioned
about why she had even been converted, since she had retained her sinful
habits, noted, "I don't know why it was I got converted, because I had
been doing nearly everything they told me I ought not to do. I danced,
played cards, and done just like I wanted to do. I don't reckon I was so
bad, but they said I was."[63] This seeker, however, became more and more
saddened by her condition and began to enjoy her old habits less and less.
Finally she became emotionally and psychologically ill. She went on to
say, "I wasn't sick, I was just heavy." Then she "passed through this
experience [and] lost all worldly cares. The things I used to enjoy don't
interest me now." She had become a "new creature in Jesus."[64] This fun-
loving convert declared that she heard a voice while she was on a dance
floor. The voice asked, "Do you remember the promise you made to
me?"[65] The promise she had made was to discontinue her bad habits,
dancing and carousing. Other former seekers recalled having heard voices
and received revelations that prompted them to give up such habits as
dancing and fiddling. Such examples show that the moral mandate in this
tradition was very strong.

God Struck Me Dead!
The Moment of Truth in the Seekin' Experience

The climactic moment of the seekin' experience was the vision, or dream. The goal of the seekin' journey was to help the sinner cross over the river, often referred to as the Jordan. Many phrases and metaphors are used to express this idea, including "God struck me dead," "my dungeons shook and my chains fell off," "dying," and "comin' through." These accent the centrality of the experience of transformation, or being born again, within the seekin' process. No theme is more dominant in the pray's house spirit than this. In my interviews and in the narratives that I have examined, there is no singular type of vision; nor is there a specific method for attaining the vision. For some persons, the vision was literally a dream that took place while they were asleep. Others, however, had their visions during the day, as they went about their chores. Still others "came through" as they worshiped in a public setting.

While the method of reaching the climax of the seekin' journey was not always the same, the goal was: being "born again."[66] The spiritual journey did not end without this experience. One of the narratives notes: "I kept on until I asked the Lord, if he had converted me, to show me a beautiful star out of a cloudy sky. This was done, and I saw a star in the daytime shining out of a cloudy sky. I know I have got it, and hell and its forces can't make me turn back."[67] The presence of the "beautiful star" in a "cloudy sky" was an affirmation of God's gift of life to the seeker, a clear indication that the seeker had indeed reached the desired goal. Mechal Sobel's analysis of the language that slaves used in describing how they "came through" is fascinating, as it demonstrates even more strongly the degree to which slaves expected that their seekin' would lead to a new sense of personal identity. In examining African American religious visions, including those described in Johnson's *God Struck Me Dead*, he notes several common characteristics, all of which relate to the uniqueness of black religious consciousness:

(1) the concept of the two selves, the "little me" and the "big me" permeating the whole vision structure; (2) the detailed journey or travels of the soul from Hell to Heaven; (3) the appearance of a little (white) man as guide on this journey; and (4) the visual description of Heaven and God, with its emphasis on whiteness.[68]

There is, as Sobel describes it, a "before" and an "after" dimension to the seekin' process, one referring to the individual's life prior to conversion and the other denoting life after conversion (after having seen the vision).[69] We note this in the following quote:

When I died, I died at hell's dark door. I looked around me, and I saw a ladder let down from the top of a house. He told me I's have to rise and follow him. I rose and stepped on the ladder and didn't stop till I reached the top. He told me he was my Father and I was his child. "Go and go in my name," he said.[70]

This narrative actually begins with God's demand that the seeker must "die" to have peace. The experience of death was symbolic of the individual's journey from the old life of sin to a new life of righteousness, as the seeker "journeyed on and came in sight of a beautiful green pasture and a beautiful mansion. . . . I don't know how I left, but I do know how I went to heaven."[71] The nature of the journey might vary from narrative to narrative and person to person, but the ingredient in these visions, for our purposes, is the idea of radical change and transformation of the individual. The crossing-over experience that we referenced above from Maggie Russell's testimony is also illustrative of this point, bringing together several of the other themes in Sobel's paradigm.

But I stayed there until the Lord talked to me in the Spirit and this night in the Spirit he came to me. I was on one side of the river, and I could not come cross the river, because there was water. And we were not supposed to walk into the water. And I said, "How I gonna git cross dat water?" And he said, when I looked back [sic]. And I looked up at him and there was this white man on a milk white horse. And I looked up and his eyes were so strong. And I tried to look in his eyes, but my eyes were too weak, I couldn't take it. His eyes were so strong. Jesus has a very strong eye. And he didn't mean for me to see into his eye, but he was talking to me. But I tried to look him in the eye. He took me by my hand. He reached down and took me by my hand. I do not know how I git through dat water. I don't know whether I walk on dat water or walked through dat water. But he lead me, he lead me across. And he said, "Go tell Peter Singleton to baptize you. Tell your Pastor to baptize you, in the Name of the Father, Son, and the Holy Ghost. And he say everything will be alright.[72]

Again, most of the dominant themes are here: crossing over the river, seeing a vision of a white man who assists the seeker in crossing the river, the direct assurance to the seeker that she had indeed been set free. We also note the presence of the vision itself, as one aspect of the entire experience, and the direction to the seeker to reenter her sociospiritual community as a full participant. The new self would now be qualified to join the church, as evidenced by the command to be baptized.

Russell's experience came to her while she was officially seekin' the Lord in the wilderness (actually under a tree in her yard); but, as I have noted, often individuals came through as a result of a dream. One South Carolinian, Louise White, describes her experience of being compelled to seek the Lord in a particular room in her house, where someone had died the previous day. This was a test of her commitment to the process, her willingness to take instruction, and her faith:

> And I say Lord please Lord I want a dream. And he gave me a dream. And I stayed in that room until day clean. And the next day they bring me again and I bin in a creek, where they catch crab, you know. And they been catching the crab. And one part of the creek, there was a flood tide coming in. And a lady was on the other side and she said come on cross. And I said I cant get cross. And she said the tide came in pretty fast and it can catch you under your throat. . . . And I put this same foot here down in the soft mud. And den they said, don't turn that side, say keep to the middle and when you get to the end stand up.[73]

The element of the dream is offered in White's experience. Moreover, her vision is distinguished from Russell's in that the human figure who mediates her dream is a woman rather than a man. In instances where a supernatural being or object is present in the dream, that being is often called God, Jesus, or the name of another spiritual person; if there is a human mediator in the dream, that figure is more often than not a male. There are other religious objects that are almost always white or very bright, and in most of the visions the seeker is sent away with an audible message of assurance indicating that she or he has indeed "come through."[74]

The individualistic strand in the narratives is certainly maintained in these visions. One must be reminded, however, of the broader context within which the visions took place. While the language and the events depicted in most of the narratives that I have studied are indeed very personal and one might say privatistic, one must look at another aspect of them in order to maintain the dialectical tension between the communal and individualistic themes. To begin with, we should remember that persons who engaged in seekin' the Lord never did so in isolation. It was always done in response to either external pressure (from the church, the pray's house, the community, or God) or internally, as a result of the individual's feelings and experiences. In either case, the individual did not begin the seekin' process without the guidance and direct instruction of someone from the church, pray's house, or community. It is within this context that we might speak of the role of the spiritual mentor, spiritual mother, the elder, deacon, pray's house leader, or seekin' mother.[75] Persons known by these titles were given the task of helping to guide the seeker through the seekin' process and indeed to interpret his or her dream. Whether it was to validate a personal experience for the individual, to testify before the church on his or her behalf, or to support the seeker's testimony in the pray's house, the distinctive, intermediary role of the mentor was maintained.

An example of a mentor's personal validation of a dream or vision is seen in the following instance, in which a daughter shares her experience with her mother:

Give me that good old-time religion. This I sang all the rest of the day, and I felt a burning in my heart, and a great burden seemed to have left me. I told my mother what had happened. She kissed me many times and told me that I had been converted, and I went my way rejoicing.[76]

In this case the mother's response was enough to convince the young woman that she had indeed been converted. This description does not give great details on the seeking mother's role, but it clearly demonstrates that she helps to interpret the dream.[77]

The ultimate test of the authenticity of a vision or dream took place when the seeker was examined by the board of deacons, in the case of the church, or by the pray's house leaders. In each context the role of the mentor was central. Howard Thurman's classic story of his first appeal to join his Mount Bethel Baptist Church gives us a sense of how this process worked. Having reached the appropriate age and having had the experience requisite for church membership, Thurman went before the board of deacons of the church to express his desire for baptism and full church membership. But he was at first rejected because he was unable to convince the deacons that he had indeed been converted. As he explained, "They examined me, and I answered their questions. When they had finished, the chairman asked, 'Howard, why do you come before us?' I said, 'I want to be a Christian.' Then the chairman said, 'But you must come before us after you have been converted and have already become a Christian.' " The chairman then sent the twelve-year-old lad away with the following admonishment, "You better get yourself straightened out, Howard. Come back when you can *tell us* of your conversion."[78] This event shows how, in the folk religious tradition that we have described in this study, a true conversion experience is expected to be accompanied by sufficient signs and insights to allow the individual to communicate the experience to others. Thurman obviously could not convince the deacons that he had indeed "come through." Thus he went home dejected and told Nancy Ambrose, his spiritual mentor, teacher, and grandmother, what had happened. And knowing of her grandson's experiences and faith, she returned to the church and interceded on his behalf. Inviting herself into their deacons' meeting, she said: "How dare you turn this boy down? He is a Christian and was one long before he came to you today. Maybe you did not *understand his words*, but shame on you if you do not know his heart. Now you take this boy into the church right now—before you close this meeting!"[79] Without hesitation, the deacons acquiesced to her demand and accepted Howard Thurman into the church, allowing him to be baptized the following Sunday.

Two primary facts emerge from Ambrose's audacious testimony. First, we clearly see her filling the role that all mentors played for their seekers; she interpreted his experience. And she could do so because she had been the principal nurturer of his faith. The deacons' rejection of her grandson was tantamount to a rejection of her wisdom and spiritual insight, for she was a witness to the depths of his faith.[80] Second, Ambrose's audacious confrontation with the leaders of her church raises a question about the significant role of the "seekin' mother" and other women of faith who helped to shape the spiritual ethos of the pray's house tradition. While, as we have noted, there were isolated instances in which women were not allowed to lead the pray's houses, their status as seekin' mothers, the women who taught and interpreted the visions, dreams, and other religious experiences of young seekers, was universally recognized in the slave quarters, and this tradition continues down to the present. While my findings are inconclusive on the number of persons who had male mentors as opposed to female mentors, it is clear that women played a dominant role. The role of the seekin' mother was critical, and her power was based totally on the strength of her age, respect in the community, and spiritual insights and other gifts.[81] The requirements in the pray's house were the same as those in the churches; there, too, seekers who had really "come through" had to tell all the things they had seen and heard.[82] In so doing, they validated their own experience and helped to strengthen the role of the mentor.

Conclusion

If the pray's house and seekin' traditions are as crucial to the formation of black religious faith as I have suggested them to be, it seems that they are of particular significance to what is going on today in African

American religious thought in general and to black and womanist theologies in particular. The question of the significance of black folk religion in writing black theology is not a new issue. Back at the earliest stages of the development of black theology, this subject, emerging primarily in reaction to the writings of James H. Cone, received quite a bit of attention. In recent years many younger African American scholars—black theologians and womanist writers—have taken to heart the task of appropriating black folk religious practices into their constructive theological projects. Among the newer works in this area are some to which I have already made reference. I am impressed with Theophus H. Smith's *Conjuring Culture*,[83] Dwight N. Hopkins and George C. L. Cummings's *Cut Loose*, Hopkins's *Shoes That Fit Our Feet*, Delores Williams's *Sisters in the Wilderness*, Emilie M. Townes's *A Troubling in My Soul*, Riggins Earl's *Dark Symbols, Obscure Signs*, and earlier Charles Long's *Significations*, to name only a few. (Long's work is an exception here because he belongs to the first generation of black theologians, but his collection of articles was not published until 1986.) Each of these texts gives us a sense of how African American scholars are appropriating the narratives, folk beliefs, and spiritual experiences of their forebears into their constructive theological and moral projects. It is my hope that this essay will contribute to the very creative developments that are taking place in this fertile area of African American religious scholarship.

Notes

1. This focus upon the experiences of Lowcountry South Carolinians, however, does not negate the strong parallels that might exist with African Americans from other regions of the United States or people of the diaspora throughout the Western world.

2. I have adopted the phrase pray's house spirit from the documentary *Praise House Spirit* (WTAT, Channel 24, Charleston, South Carolina, December 19, 1991). My rationale for using the rendition "pray's" as opposed to "praise" is given below. At any rate, the phrase pray's house spirit depicts both the institutional structure and the spiritual core of the pray's house, as I will address the subject in this study. The *G*, from the participle in "seekin' the Lord," is deleted to reflect the common pronunciation of the term among persons in the South Carolina Lowcountry.

3. Consider, for example, the following, all published by Orbis in Maryknoll, New York: Riggins Earl, *Dark Symbols, Obscure Signs* (1993); Dwight N. Hopkins and George C. L. Cummings, *Cut Loose Your Stammering Tongue* (1991); Dwight Hopkins, *Shoes That Fit Our Feet* (1993); Emilie M. Townes, *A Trou-*

bling in My Soul (1993); and Delores Williams, *Sisters in the Wilderness* (1993). Other relevant texts—both with a more anthropological emphasis—include Walter F. Pitts Jr., *Old Ship of Zion* (New York: Oxford University Press, 1993); and Peter Goldsmith, *When I Rise Crying Holy* (New York: AMS Press, 1989). All these books, with the exception of Goldsmith's, represent the continuing treatment of this subject, begun much earlier in black theology with the work of Charles Long and Cecil W. Cone. See Long, *Significations* (Philadelphia: Fortress, 1986); and Cone, *The Identity Crisis in Black Theology* (Nashville: African Methodist Episcopal Church, 1975). Other pertinent studies will be noted below.

4. Lawton notes that the use of the "praise house" rendering was more common among white scholars. A casual observation of the current scholarship in this area, however, will reveal that this remains the rendition of choice for most scholars today. Nevertheless, my interviews reveal that the pray's house rendering is still preferred among residents. Thus my choice of the latter. See Samuel Lawton, "The Religious Life of Coastal and Sea Island Negroes" (Ph.D. dissertation, George Peabody College for Teachers, 1939), 54–56; see also Patricia Guthrie, "Catching Sense: The Meaning of Plantation Membership on St. Helena Island, South Carolina" (Ph.D. dissertation, University of Rochester, 1977); and Margaret Washington Creel, *A Peculiar People: Slave Religion and Community Culture among the Gullahs* (New York: New York University Press, 1988).

5. Lawton has noted that the reference to the pray's houses gatherings as class meetings can be traced back to the influence of the Methodist "class system." Methodists have historically broken down their membership into classes for the purpose of creating intimacy and doing more effective shepherding. My experiences as a resident of the South Carolina Lowcountry indicate that many individuals in this region today refer to their pray's houses as classrooms. Research indicates that many Sea Islanders currently refer to their pray's houses as classrooms. The influence of the African Methodist Episcopal Church in the South Carolina Lowcountry is also significant in this regard. See Lawton, "Religious Life," 60.

6. Note the expressions of these ideas in the present volume, particularly in the essays by Spencer, Johnson, and Carr-Hamilton.

7. See, for example, Creel, *A Peculiar People*; Eugene Genovese, *Roll, Jordan, Roll: The World the Slaves Made* (New York: Vintage Books, 1976); and George P. Rawick, *From Sundown to Sunup: The Making of the Black Community* (Westport, Conn.: Greenwood Press, 1972).

8. This description is quoted in Guy and Candie Carawan, *Ain't You Got a Right to the Tree of Life*, rev. ed. (Athens: University of Georgia Press, 1988), 74.

9. Like other aspects of the African American traditions of the South, the brush arbor phenomenon continued to thrive because many religious groups could not afford to purchase existing church buildings or build new ones. Therefore they resorted to using tents, or brush arbors, as temporary places of worship. This is particularly true of newer groups such as Holiness Pentecostals.

10. Guthrie, "Catching Sense," 88.

11. Efforts to reach slaves in this period were certainly slowed by the attempted insurrections, as laws against slave gatherings and private meetings were developed to limit such actions. An Alabama law of 1832 required that at least five "respectable slave holders" attend services where slaves were worshipping and preaching. Milton C. Sernett, *Black Religion and American Evangelicalism: White Pentecost Plantation Missions and the Flowering of Negro Christianity, 1787–1865* (Metuchen, N.J.: Scarecrow Press), 96.

12. Charles C. Jones, a Presbyterian evangelical, was perhaps the most famous white missionary to the slaves during this era. However, the growth of the Methodist Episcopal Church in the South should be viewed in relationship to its willingness to relax its earlier restrictions—dating back to the time of John Wesley—against slaveholding and allowing slaveholders to be members of their societies. Note, for example, its 1804 repeal of all restrictions against buying and selling slaves from the rules governing its societies in the Carolinas, Georgia, and Tennessee and also its 1808 decision to allow slaveholders to hold offices in its churches. See Sernett, *Black Religion*, 37.

13. She goes further to note that the members of different churches would often cooperate with each other in promoting such activities as Sunday school ministries for their children at particular pray's houses and then would later attend the churches of their choice, thus underscoring the ecumenical nature of the pray's house tradition. Guthrie, "Catching Sense," 16–17. By 1845 the Methodist Episcopal Church had sixty-one full-time mission stations, Sunday schools, and other such groups working on the plantations.

14. Titles such as elder, deacon, mother, father, and the like were honorary in southern black communities, reflecting the type of respect that was offered to older persons, church members, and persons who were otherwise esteemed for their spiritual insights and their overall behavior. Reverence for the wisdom and knowledge of the aged runs deep within the African American community. Moreover, these are not denominational titles, though they refer to titles that exist in many traditions.

15. As quoted in Creel, *A Peculiar People*, 196. Creel makes very important connections between the secret societies on the plantations, the pray's houses, the leadership class in both contexts, and the efforts of whites to evangelize on the plantation. No great inroads could be made without the goodwill of such persons.

16. Interview with Maggie Russell in the documentary *Praise House Spirit*.

17. Ibid. The days that she notes here are consistent with what I have observed in talking to people who still attend meetings on places such as Wadmalaw Island, South Carolina.

18. Lawton, "Religious Life," 62.

19. Ibid., 63.

20. Another area I have not considered in this study is the conflicts that might have emerged between pray's house activities and those of local congregations. See Guthrie, "Catching Sense," 94.

21. A more detailed discussion of the relationship between the seeking traditions of African Americans and the African rite of passage or similar traditions among other peoples of the diaspora is beyond the scope of this study. See Creel, *A Peculiar People*; and Pitts, *Old Ship of Zion*, for more information on these topics.

22. Guthrie, "Catching Sense," 21. Note that in the specific politicoreligious worldview being described here, only the children are, as Guthrie says, taken fully through this process of "catching sense." And this was reserved for children from primary relationships, those who were brought up in one's own household.

23. Lawton, for example, noted that twelve of fifty-five adults that he examined listed this as their reason for seeking membership in the pray's house. See his "Religious Life," 136–38.

24. Guthrie, "Catching Sense," 90.

25. Lawton, "Religious Life," 71. One connection here that is worth exploring is the degree to which the leadership of women in the houses corresponded to the degree of denominational control and the differences in denominational polities regarding female leadership and ministry. If my hunch is fully supported, it would seem that there would be a greater percentage of female leadership in areas where Methodists are dominant—they have a longer tradition of allowing females into the ordained ministry and other positions of church leadership—than in areas where the dominant religious communities are Baptist. In the South Carolina Lowcountry, interestingly, the AME Church is the largest tradition.

26. Ibid., 95. It is beyond the scope of this study to note the relationship between the prayer bands that we are discussing here and the "bands" of prayer worriers that Bishop Daniel Alexander Payne discovered and so detested in the African Methodist Episcopal churches in the North, only one decade removed from slavery. See his discussion of this issue in his *Recollections of Seventy Years*, first published 1886 (New York: Arno Press and the New York Times, 1969), 253–55. Vennie Deas-Moore's interview with Louise White of Awendaw, South Carolina, February 8, 1989 (unpublished transcription, McKissick Museum, University of South Carolina, Columbia, South Carolina).

27. See for example, C. Eric Lincoln and Lawrence Mamiya, *The Black Church in the African American Experience* (Durham, N.C.: Duke University Press, 1990). The authors provide a substantial amount of information on the traditions, practices, and demographics of African American congregations throughout the country.

28. See also Guthrie, "Catching Sense," 109.

29. Lawton, "Religious Life," 141.

30. Vennie Deas-Moore's interview with Dorothy Franklin of the South Carolina Lowcountry, April 10, 1989, 15–16 (unpublished transcription).

31. See Charles G. Finney, *Lectures on Revivals of Religion* (Virginia Beach, Va.: CBN University Press, 1978), 280. Note also the discussion of Finney's methods in William McLoughlin, *Modern Revivalism: Charles Grandison Finney to Billy Graham* (New York: Roland Press, 1959).

32. Creel, *A Peculiar People*, 286.
33. The protracted meetings were the extended revival campaigns employed by evangelicals, sometimes for weeks on end. They went hand in hand with the anxious meetings and other innovations created by nineteenth-century evangelical revivalists, all of which were designed to generate more converts. See McLoughlin, *Modern Revivalism*.
34. See Finney, *Revivals of Religion*, 274. McLoughlin provides an excellent analysis of this tradition in his *Modern Revivalism*.
35. Creel has made the case for understanding the seekin' experience as a rite of initiation. See Creel, *A Peculiar People*, 286–89. W. E. B. DuBois, *The Souls of Black Folk* (New York: New American Library, 1969). An extremely important connection might be made here between the African initiation rites, the seekin' rituals of Afro-Caribbean religious groups, and the folk religious practices of African American southerners. An examination of this connection is beyond the scope of this study, but see Creel's treatment of this issue in her *Peculiar People*, chapter 9, and in her chapter in Joseph E. Holloway, ed., *Africanisms in American Culture* (Bloomington: Indiana University Press, 1990). See also Walter Pitts, *Old Ship of Zion*; and Clifton Johnson, *God Struck Me Dead* (Philadelphia: Pilgrim Press, 1969), vii f. For a good sampling of such discussions see Holloway, *Africanisms in American Culture*.
36. Lawton's study is the most thorough analysis of the South Carolina seekin' tradition. Much of my treatment of the subject draws upon his research.
37. I also make generous references to such secondary sources as Creel's *Peculiar People* and Mechal Sobel's *Trabelin' On: The Slave Journey to an Afro-Baptist Faith* (Westport, Conn.: Greenwood Press, 1979). The interviews that I make use of are all taken from individuals from the South Carolina Lowcountry. These texts and interviews provide a sense of the diversity of seekin' models.
38. As quoted in Creel, *A Peculiar People*, 287.
39. Lawton's study reveals that the average age of South Carolina seekers—those who began as children—was roughly 12.1 years; for adults, however, the age was 19 ("Religious Life," 131).
40. Quoted in Johnson, *God Struck Me Dead*, 165.
41. Ibid., 145.
42. Ibid., 147.
43. Ibid., 143.
44. Lawton, "Religious Life," 143.
45. Deas-Moore, interview with Louise White of Awendaw, South Carolina, February 18, 1989, 24.
46. See Turner, *The Ritual Process: Structure and Antistructure* (Ithaca: Cornell University Press, 1977).
47. Interview with Maggie Russell in the documentary *Praise House Spirit*.
48. Howard Thurman, *With Head and Heart* (New York: Harcourt Brace Jovanovich, 1979), 18.
49. In reading such documents as *God Struck Me Dead*, other conversion narratives, and interviews with many Gullahs of today, one is immediately struck by the

frequency of seekers' references to having to journey through water when they are coming through.

50. Interview with Maggie Russell in the documentary *Praise House Spirit.*

51. The influence of the pray's houses that continues to exist in the South Carolina Lowcountry pales when compared to that of pray's houses of the antebellum period and postwar period. Nevertheless, they continue to exist, with a few older members participating in their activities. One of the more noted ones is the Moving Star Hall on Johns Island, South Carolina. This pray's house was built on the island around 1914. It has since been a central place for community gatherings, prayer meetings, and the like. See a discussion of this in Carawan, *Ain't You Got a Right to the Tree of Life*, 74. My concern is to note the institutional function of the pray's houses in the South Carolina Lowcountry communities. They are one key aspect of the social world created by African Americans and part of their self-made religious environments in the South, as I have noted above.

52. I have found this theme equally strong in the literature on slave religious experiences across the South. Persons familiar with the works of Howard Thurman, one of the most prolific African American religious writers of this century, will note the strength of his nature-centered spirituality. He often wrote of how it was shaped by his long forays, as a young person in Daytona, into the thick woods and his journeys along the Atlantic Coast. See especially his autobiography, *With Head and Heart.*

53. Interview with Maggie Russell in the documentary *Praise House Spirit.*

54. Johnson, *God Struck Me Dead*, 126.

55. Sobel, *Trabelin' On*, 111.

56. The majority of individuals portrayed in Lawton's study did their seekin' in the wilderness and choose to use the specific language of wilderness to describe their experience rather than terms such as field, woods, yard, tree, and the like. Most adults did their seekin' outdoors, whereas the children most often did theirs either in their homes or in their churches ("Religious Life," 145–48). It is of particular interest (but a topic beyond the scope of this study) to note, especially in the *God Struck Me Dead* narratives, the preponderance of emphasis on the journey as an experience that takes the individual from the "west" to the "east," with the east, more often than not, being symbolic of spiritual freedom and obedience to God. We might speculate about whether this has some reference either to the Underground Railroad or to the idea of going back east, ultimately to Africa. Both notions would have made sense to slaves from Tennessee. See for example 21, 63–64, 66, 100–101, 114.

57. Lawton, "Religious Life," 148.

58. Johnson, *God Struck Me Dead*, 123.

59. Ibid., p. 150. See Genovese, *Roll, Jordan, Roll*, for a more complete discussion of this point; note especially book 2.

60. Johnson, *God Struck Me Dead*, 123.

61. Ibid.

62. The desire for some type of interaction with pray's house and church leaders

and members was also listed as a major reason some people began to seek the Lord.

63. Johnson, *God Struck Me Dead*, 111.
64. Ibid.
65. Ibid.
66. See Sobel, *Trabelin' On*, chapter 5.
67. Johnson, *God Struck Me Dead*, 128.
68. Sobel, *Trabelin' On*, 113.
69. Ibid. Sobel indicates that there is a "little me/big me" motif in the conversion narratives that can be traced back to certain African views about the human soul. But the key here is to note that it points to the change that was supposed to take place within individuals as a result of their conversion.
70. Sobel, *Trabelin' On*, 167.
71. Ibid., 48.
72. Interview with Maggie Russell in the documentary *Praise House Spirit*.
73. Vennie Deas-Moore, interview with Louise White, 24.
74. Sobel has done a careful analysis of the color symbolism in Johnson's *God Struck Me Dead* narratives that clearly has implications for studies such as this present one. She has connected the significance of the color white to the symbolism in African traditional religions, thus giving it a more authentic, African, point of origin as opposed to attributing the slave's use and African American use of white images and symbols to their conscious or unconscious forms of self-hatred. See Sobel, *Trabelin' On*, 108–22.
75. The seekin' mother is also referred to as a "spiritual mother" by the persons in the churches and communities who respected her. See Lawton, "Religious Life," 1939.
76. Johnson, *God Struck Me Dead*, 126.
77. The informality of the mother's role as interpreter of her daughter's dream does not lessen the significance of this office as we have tried to understand it for the purposes of this study. In the more formal relationships between seeker and mentor, there would be a period of teaching. Moreover, in some traditions, the seeker's vision would not be validated until she or he had seen or heard in a dream a secret word that God had given to the spiritual mentor. See Lawton, "Religious Life," 140.
78. Thurman, *With Head and Heart*, 18.
79. Ibid.
80. Lawton provides a strong basis for this thesis in his discussion of the strong role of mentors and their influence in presenting a seeker's case to the pray's house and church communities. Lawton, "Religious Life," 140–43.
81. The respect that individuals had for such persons is further indicated by the fact that most mentors were selected by seekers as a result of some revelational experience. In a future study I will look more carefully at this area as a means of understanding the role of women in southern African American religious communities. I will look specifically at the symbolic connection between the role of the seekin' mother and that of the church mother, a role of signifi-

cant power in most African American traditions to which there is no counter-
part in the white community.

82. Lawton, "Religious Life," 128. The role of the spiritual mentors was very
significant on plantations where secret societies were dominant and where
there was a strong tradition of slave preachers. See Creel, *A Peculiar People*,
285–87; Genovese, *Roll, Jordan, Roll*; and Sernett, *Black Religion* for discussions of these two factors, which were particularly significant in shaping the
folk traditions about which we are concerned.

83. Theophus H. Smith, *Conjuring Culture: Biblical Formations of Black America*
(New York: Oxford University Press, 1994).

The Rhythms of Black Folks

Jon Michael Spencer

In many traditional African societies the drum is a sacred instrument possessing supernatural power that enables it to summon the gods into ritual communion with the people. In some societies drums are regarded as deities whose voices are the percussive sounds that emanate. These drums, and all drums of lesser sacred status, perform a requisite function in the music accompanying ritualistic dance, for with the articulations of these instruments drummers seduce dancers into a state of ready fervor and mobilize the spirits into possessive action. The rhythm that does the seducing is characterizable as *African rhythm*, the singular noun intended to represent the common aspects of rhythm shared by most societies of continental Africa: first, its sacrality; and second, its multimetricity, cross-rhythms, asymmetrical patterning, and call and response, all articulated improvisatorily and percussively, especially upon the drum, and customarily concretized in dance.

Because the drums that articulate this African rhythm are important voices in African ritual and cosmology, it must have been a cultural shock when the drum had difficulty surviving some parts of the African diaspora. While there was continued use of the drum in the West Indies and South America, the instrument was essentially disallowed in North America by legal mandate because of the fears slaveholders had of its ability to "talk." But while the use of the drum was deferred in the diaspora, the drumbeats of Africa endured the slave factories and the middle passage and were sold along with the captive Africans on the auction blocks of the New World. Those drumbeats sat silent in many a gallery of white Protestant and Catholic churches until they could "steal away" and release themselves without reproach in the physical concretizations of those who had carried the rhythm in the blood and bones and souls beneath their flesh.

African rhythm was the essential African remnant—the acme of Africanism. Certainly the drum was a sacred instrument, theologically pertinent to African ritual, but it was not so crucial an instrument that its absence prevented the continuation of such Africa-wide rituals as the ring shout. In the New World this African dance was comprised of shuffling in a counterclockwise circle to the beat of song with the feet hardly taken from the floor. One white observer of shouting on Saint Helena Island, South Carolina, noted in 1862 that three men stood apart and sang and clapped while those who followed one another in the ring picked up tempo and momentum: "They began slowly, a few going around a[nd] more gradually joining in, the song getting faster and faster till at last only the most marked part of the refrain is sung and the shuffling, stamping, and clapping gets furious." The observer concluded by saying that the floor, which swayed regularly to the time of the music, shook so much that it seemed dangerous.[1] Around the same time and on the same South Carolina island, another white observer noticed that during the circular shuffling, which was usually but not always accompanied by singing, the dancers displayed a jerking motion that agitated their entire bodies.[2] Still another noted that there was a joining of hands by the ring dancers.[3] In each description of the shout's choreography, the dance is accompanied by percussive rhythm articulated corporeally, a manifestation that the dancers sometimes referred to as "getting the power" and being "filled with the Spirit." Thus the ring shout illustrates that in the absence of the drum, other sources of rhythm were capable of summoning the spirits and mobilizing them into possessive action on the people.

In addition to the ring shout, which during slavery generally occurred without the knowledge of whites, creolized African dance styles maintained in the secret and public secular dance arenas were also harbingers of African rhythms. In these dance arenas the movement motifs that were African were probably reinforced when newly imported Africans exerted a cultural influence on the plantations.[4] After slavery the African dance motifs in the secular dances found their way into the dances done in the jook joints in small towns of the rural South.[5] Since the jook was the only dance arena that accommodated the emerging culture of southern black freedpersons, it served as the common ground for the mixing of any remaining strains of African cultures along with those creole Africanisms that developed during slavery.[6] The dance styles of the jooks, which served rural populations of blacks, were proliferated among traveling black performers in the southern tent and medicine shows.[7] During the great migration, southern blacks brought these dance styles north. As the jook and its first urban progeny in the North, the honky-tonk, evolved into the urban after-hours joint, rent party, and black-owned club, the dances began losing their rural characteristics, and the remnant of group dancing diminished in favor of individualized and increasingly sexualized partner dancing.[8]

But the African movement motifs, which were the corporeal concretizations of the creole African rhythms, continued. The dances nurtured on the plantations and later in the jooks and beyond (in the jook continuum) were comprised of recycled movement motifs that could be traced back to Africa. For example, the dance called the itch, which can be traced back to the Winti people in Suriname (whose dancers tug at their clothing as though scratching), was incorporated into the breakaway of the lindy hop by the late 1940s and returned as an embellishment to rhythm and blues dances of the 1950s.[9] The plantation dance called wringin' and twistin' became the basis of the twist, and the leg gestures of the Charleston appeared during the late 1950s and early 1960s in the dance called the mashed potatoes.[10] The hip gestures of the black bottom appeared as an embellishment in the lindy hop and jitterbug, later in the mooche, and even later in the four corners of the late 1960s and early 1970s.[11] The camel walk, which can be traced back to Ghana, is a step similar to an Ashanti funeral dance called the Adowa.[12] Even the contemporary soul-train line had its beginnings among many West African ethnic groups.[13]

While the religious places of worship were thus certainly important locations for the creolization of African rhythm during and beyond antebellum times, the jook continuum was perhaps the portentous place of rhythmic creolization that has forever left its impression on the culture of modern times. As the philosopher Alain Locke puts it, slavery may have robbed Africans of their ancestral gift of fine craftsmanship, but their artistic urges continued to flow into the channels of movement, song, and speech, and the body itself became the primary artistic instrument of black people.[14] Locke's contemporary of the early part of the twentieth century, composer R. Nathaniel Dett, the well-known arranger of spirituals, identified call-and-response and the pentatonic scale as prominent elements that reveal the African roots of black music. But Dett also said it was obvious that rhythm is what establishes the crucial link between the music of black Americans and that of their African forebears, rhythm that is "reincarnated and re-christened" with each generation as syncopation, ragtime, jazz, and swing.[15] Composer William Grant Still, a friend of both Dett and Locke, said he heard African rhythm not only in the spirituals and the blues but also in the Cuban rumba, the Brazilian samba, the Colombian bambuco, and the Haitian merengue.[16]

Thus the drumbeats of Africa endured the slave factories and the middle passage and were sold along with the captive Africans on the auction blocks of the New World. Those drumbeats, creolized and corporealized, survived urbanization as well, which robbed blacks of the environment of nature—their chief conduit in the rural South, as in Africa, into the spirit world. The drumbeats of Africa, creolized and corporealized, also survived industrialization, with its staid rhythms that, though percussive, beat counter to the asymmetry, multimetricism, and improvi-

sation of African time. Having thus survived in the black folk and popular
genres of music and dance, these drumbeats found their way into the
sophisticated classical compositions and vocal performances of such musicians as R. Nathaniel Dett, William Grant Still, Roland Hayes, Marian
Anderson, and Dorothy Maynor. The survival of old African rhythms into
modern times is the reason Alain Locke was able to say of these black
artists that, though they are thoroughly modern and their thoughts "wear
the uniform of the age," their hearts yet "beat a little differently."[17]
Locke is also writing of these artists when he comments further about the
kernel of African rhythm sprouting anew in the artistic soils of myriad
diasporan lands:

> This racial mastery of rhythm is one characteristic that seems
> never to have been lost, whatever else was, and it has made and
> kept the Negro a musician by nature and a music-maker by instinct.
> When customs were lost and native cultures cut off in the rude trans-
> plantings of slavery . . . , underneath all, rhythm memories and
> rhythmic skill persisted to fuse with and transform whatever new
> mode of expression the Negro took on. For just as music can be
> carried without words, so rhythm can be carried without the rest of
> the music system; so intimately and instinctively is it carried. From
> this mustard-seed the whole structure of music can sprout anew.
> From a kernel of rhythm, African music has sprouted in strange
> lands, spread out a rootage of folk-dance and folk song, and then
> gone through the whole cycle of complete musical expression as far
> as soil and cultural conditions have permitted.[18]

Despite the fact that urbanization removed the urban North from the
environment of nature with its connection to the spirit world, the hearts
of the Negro Renaissance artists of the first and second postslavery generations still beat a little differently. In the case of the aforementioned composers and performers, it was the spirituals (for Still it was also the blues)
that had left an impression upon them. Dett and Still recalled that they
had heard their grandmothers sing spirituals when they were children.
When Dett, as a student at Oberlin Conservatory of Music, heard the slow
movement of Antonin Dvorak's *American Quartet*, containing melodies
from the spirituals, his heart beat a little differently. As he said in one of
his essays, under the fitting heading "The Singing Dead," it seemed that
he had suddenly heard the sweet voice of his long-departed grandmother
calling across the years. In a rush of emotion that stirred his spirit to its
very heart, he recalled, the meaning of the songs that had given her soul
such peace was revealed to him.[19] Still must have had a similar heartfelt

experience, for he remembered that his maternal grandmother, who lived in his mother's home in Little Rock, Arkansas, used to sing spirituals all day long. He also heard the spirituals and saw individuals doing the religious dance called the shout when he and his mother once visited a rural church. At that time the histrionic display struck him as humorous, but he later drew artistically from the experience of having heard this black music at its authentic source.[20]

What Still probably heard at that church and remembered was not simply the African rhythms of the singing and the shouting but also the rhythms of the preaching. The African rhythms of black preaching comprise the single ingredient that gives the melodiousness of the traditional black sermonry both its momentum and its momentousness. Even contemporary black preachers who have drawn artistically from the experience of having heard black music at its authentic source continue to pursue the skill of improvisatorily fitting their phrases and sentences into quasi-metrical units. They accomplish this by squeezing together and stretching out words in the same way that is done by the rap artist (the black preacher's contemporary linguistic kin), and they often accompany this quasi-metered articulation by striking the lectern or stomping the foot. Thus, the "drumming" of traditional black preaching (like black rapping) includes kinetic, linguistic, and metric manifestations, which together create a polyphonic multimetricity equivalent to that in African rhythm.

It was probably their having experienced some aspect of traditional black singing, shouting, and preaching that led the Negro Renaissance artists to arrange and sing the spirituals and led them back to the South to collect these folk songs at their authentic source. Dorothy Maynor recalled that though her teacher and mentor Dett was born in Canada and raised in the North, he had a yearning to learn about life in the South.[21] Maynor herself, and others such as Roland Hayes, also spent time in that ritual region gathering black folk songs from the nature that grew them. Hayes, in fact, went even further and spent substantial time studying African music. Having acquired a degree of technical knowledge about the music, he also had hopes of one day going to Africa for more study.[22] Even though the Negro Renaissance composers and performers chose to work within the classical musical genres and had mastered the requisite skills to do so, their treatment of the spirituals was by no means despiritualized, as many white critics believed. The same holds true for Still's treatment of the blues.

Though African rhythms wore the uniform of the age in the music of the Negro Renaissance artists, the drumbeats of Africa, though creolized, still beat a little differently. Indeed, the continuum of African rhythm in the New World remained so strong that this might have been the answer to a question W. E. B. Du Bois raised: "Since the concept of race has so changed and presented so much of contradiction . . . as I face Africa I ask myself: what is it between us that constitutes a tie which I can feel better than I can explain?"[23]

To summarize, so that we can return full circle to the ring shout for another level of analysis, the diaspora generally took the drum away from the enslaved Africans of North America, but it did not take their rhythm. With the drum deferred in the diaspora, the percussive rhythms of "home" could still be manifested corporeally in handclapping, foot-stomping, and bodypatting. When corporealized in that most crucial African retention—dancing—the creole African rhythms produced, among other African-influenced choreographies, the ring shout. The ring shout holds an especially important place in the New World continuum of African rhythm because it was evidently closely connected to the African trickster figure. Historian Sterling Stuckey says, "Since tricksters, most notably the hare, pervade much of black Africa, as does the ring ceremony honoring the ancestors, and since the trickster and the circle are associated not only in South America where Africans were enslaved but in North American slavery as well, the evidence implies a wide association of the two in black Africa and, consequently, among numerous African ethnic groups in America."[24] The reason the association of the trickster with the ring shout is so important to me as I attempt to comprehend the momentousness of black music is that I interpret the trickster as the deity most representative of both the ritual place of rhythm-induced extradependence and the personality of that extradependence. Like the tricksters of Africa and the New World who are embodiments of synchronous duplicity—both spiritual and sexual, sacred and profane—the ritual place and personality of rhythm-induced extradependence are characterized by permissibility. This ritual place comprises experiences of gathering, greeting, singing, testifying, dance, trance, and collapse that are simultaneously spiritual and sexual, sacred and profane.

It is in such rhythmic spaces at the ritual "crossroads" of the trickster that a deep therapy of spiritual reintensification transpires. Perhaps the best way to describe this power that seems to be generated in betwixt-and-between spaces of repressively "structured" societies is by reference to what anthropologist Victor Turner calls "antistructure" and its product, "communitas." Communitas breaks in through the cracks of structure in liminality, at the edges of structure in marginality, from beneath structure in inferiority[25]—and, I might add, breaks in from above structure in spirituality. I surmise that the power that black people are able to generate corporeally in those spaces within, beneath, beside, and above suppressive structures of society—those crossroad places that the trickster, because of his synchronous duplicity, is able to forge out for ritual—is the same power that black music makers of the folk and popular genres are able to glean through embodiment of the trickster personality. This is exactly what black music makers have done. Having first emulated the tricksters that they thematized in their tales, ballads, and blues, they eventually began to live those "tricky" lives.

I am suggesting that it is not just the regular return to religious ritual (where the permissive spirit of the trickster dwells) that is so crucial to black people's maintaining their religious cosmology and cultural peculiarities, but that there is a return to what I would like to call the trickster's rhythms. This return to and from African rhythms must therefore be understood as what philosopher Martin Buber calls the "two primary metacosmical movements of the world."[26] As social scientist Bruce Reed explains, the lives of religious people are characterized by an oscillation or swing between daily human intradependence and spiritual extradependence.[27] I suppose this means that an atheist (if there is such a person) is one who does not "swing," given the spiritual lives of black people as comprised of a normative oscillation from intradependence to ritual locations of rhythm. In these ritual places, whether they are sacred or secular, rhythm provides both the pulse and the impulse hand in hand; and the experiences of gathering, greeting, singing, testifying, dance, trance, and collapse give the people the reintensified strength they need to face again the structured and often oppressive workaday world.

I believe that the reintensifying rhythms in these ritual places leave their psychophysiological impression on each "worshipper," so that the impression appears in the black community as "style" or "soul." When well-rounded, the impression becomes grace; when well-developed, charisma. When performed, it might be jazz; or when articulated, rap. African diaspora scholar Leonard Barrett suggests further that the impression of African rhythms also results in the self-confidence that fuels protest and insurrection:

The restless rhythm of the African soul . . . was obvious to the white man from the day the Africans came ashore in the Caribbean until the day Emancipation was declared. It surfaced in the drums of the Maroons in the Cockpit Mountains of Jamaica; in the conch shells of the Haitians calling the barefooted soldiers to unite against the elite French regiments "steeled" by the drums of Vodun. It became a movement bound for the African homeland under Marcus Garvey's messianic leadership and later taken up by the Rastafarians.

It escalated to a worldwide sound in the sixties in a holocaust of movements, the tremors of which still linger with us.[28]

This means that had the slave traders succeeded in breaking the spirit of their captives in those slave factories on the West coast of Africa—that is, had they contrived of a way of derhythmizing them—then there would have been no spirituals and no black church and no blues, no freedom songs and no freedom marches, no rhythm and blues and no soul and no black consciousness movement, no black theology and no rap. Had the slaveholders, in an irrational act of desperation, enacted laws strictly forbidding their slaves not only to drum but to dance, sing, preach, pray, clap, stomp, sway, even to cradle their infants in their bosoms to the rhythms of their hearts that beat a little differently—and had they gone so far as to attribute those prohibitive laws to, say, the Apostle Paul—then after a generation or two they probably would have succeeded in breaking their captives. Confiscating the drum was certainly a cultural shock to the enslaved, but to have seized their rhythms would have been the ultimate act of dehumanization, indeed de-Africanization. Without rhythm the New World descendants of the enslaved would have been a people without a cultural identity, and as rhythmless creatures, even Africans themselves might have been convinced that they had no soul. But the drumbeats of Africa endured the slave factories and the middle passage and were sold right along with the captive Africans on the auction blocks of the New World. Those drumbeats, creolized and corporealized, in turn survived urbanization and industrialization, thus solidifying a permanent place in black folk, popular, and classical culture.

Thus the answer to the question anthropological archaeologist Leland Ferguson asks about black people's source of courage in the face of the historical depravation of slavery and oppression is that blacks never forsook their reintensifying rhythms. Ferguson is already privy to the answer, for he says:

> However white Southerners and others responded to the Civil Rights Movement, one thing was true: it commanded respect. Black leaders were courageous, dignified, and articulate. But where did their strength come from? How was it created? Most whites could not say. . . . How could American Negroes—supposedly primitive at worst and poorly educated at best—gather the strength to fight the establishment and win? The answer, of course, was that beyond the eye and mind of the white majority, African American culture was vibrantly alive, and had been alive for more than three hundred years. Through that span, African Americans combined African leg-

acy with American culture, and along the way they left stories in the ground.[29]

Martin Luther King Jr. must have been one of the courageous, dignified, and articulate leaders of whom Ferguson was speaking. Having been at the forefront of freedom marches and mass meetings where music was a means of courage, King said that both the rhythm and the words of the music were sources of vibrancy among black people.[30] The words were important because they contextualized the rhythms by reflecting the specific event during the protests. But I want to argue that rhythm was the most important element. In addition to the fact that rhythm is required for the articulation of words so that those words can best convey their meaning, the real importance of rhythm is that it works at a more fundamental psychophysiological level. This is the aspect of rhythm that psychologist Carl Seashore says "gives us a feeling of power," the power to which I believe black people always oscillate in their search for extradependent re-intensification. Of this rhythm Seashore says, "The pattern once grasped, there is an assurance of ability to cope with the future. This results in . . . a motor attitude, or a projection of the self in action; for rhythm is never rhythm unless one feels that he himself is acting it, or, what may seem contradictory, that he is even carried by his own action."[31]

The points of Seashore's analysis cojoin in the actual act of marching. We could again turn to the ring shout, but let us instead use as an example the march, which during antebellum and postbellum years was a choreography that occurred at the religious meetings of blacks. According to Ella Clark, raised on her parents' plantation in Georgia, the former slaves who worshipped in the plantation church marched in pairs or in single procession to the beat of singing, and the more rhythmically involved in the music they became the more elaborate was their march. "I watched the leader as he rose in his dignity and poise," recalled Clark. "One by one his followers joined him. Perhaps Primus our blacksmith would lead a slow processional. Brer Square the preacher would 'hist' the tune."[32] Howard Odum and Guy B. Johnson attempted to look past the external features of such choreography into the thoughts of the participants. In reading their thoughts, a reading probably based on songs they either had sung or could have sung, Odum and Johnson painted the spiritual landscape that probably gave meaning to the choreography. They said that "the Negroes often imagined themselves to be the children of Israel, while their marching songs represented Moses leading them out from under the bondage of Pharaoh, or they considered themselves as marching around the wall of some besieged city. Victory would be theirs sooner or later."[33] So it would be correct to say, as King did, that together the rhythm and the words of the freedom songs were important.

However, I contend that it was rhythm that was absolutely crucial to the movement, as to the Jamaican maroons in the Cockpit Mountains and to the Haitians whose conch shells called black soldiers to unite against the French. I believe musical texts were not always necessary to give rhythm a context, for, as Odum and Johnson illustrate, a mental image could be drawn from other sources. Walter Fauntroy, another courageous and articulate leader of the civil rights movement, demonstrated this when he borrowed biblical and hymnic imagery to portray the many civil rights marches in which he participated. He said that under King's leadership black people took their concerns to the streets, and their instruments were their marching feet: "And they marched until the patter of their feet became the thunder of the marching men of Joshua, and the world rocked beneath their tread. . . . And so, the decades of the sixties, I think, will go down as a classic example of the church of God 'marching as to war with the cross of Jesus marching on before.' "[34]

Thus the answer to the question whites had as to how blacks, uneducated if not primitive, could gather the strength to fight the establishment and win was that there was something beyond the sight and thoughts of whites that was vibrantly alive in black culture: that something was African rhythms. Through his archaeological study of the earthen story of seventeenth- and eighteenth-century southern plantations, Ferguson confirms that the material culture of enslaved Africans laid the domestic foundation for a culture that gave its black adherents "power." The material culture that was African-derived—tools, pottery, basketry, dwellings, and so forth—constituted symbols of power that reinforced the views the enslaved had of themselves as Africans who were culturally distinct from their captors.[35] Ferguson says, "While many slaves may not have overtly resisted their enslavement on a day-to-day basis, most did ignore European American culture in favor of their own, and in doing so they also ignored and resisted the European American ideology that rationalized their enslavement. Archaeological research helps us see the contrast between the world the slaves built and the one they rejected."[36]

I contend that what the archaeological evidence reveals to us is that the social advances of the civil rights movement, as well as the black revolutions of the West Indies, came through a confidence derived from the African heritage of rhythm. The archaeological evidence also verifies that this rhythmic confidence was especially nurtured in the context of the religion to which it also gave rise and was part and parcel. For Ferguson says that engraved spoons and bowls excavated on Lowcountry plantation sites, evidence of African-style religious ritual, make tangible his sense that Africans brought to the Americas not only a myriad of practical skills but also aspects of their traditional spiritual beliefs.[37]

Finally, the archaeological evidence reinforces my explanation of what I think Leonard Barrett means when he says, "The drum is Africa and the drumbeats of Africa were the prime method of Africanizing the New World."[38] What Barrett seems to be saying is similar to a theology of culture, which holds that religion is all-pervasive in culture and therefore gives rise to culture. Bringing a musical hermeneutic to bear on this theology of culture, appropriate since I have already argued that rhythm and the spirit are one and the same, I am arguing that African rhythms give rise to recurrent dominant traits in all Afro-diasporan cultures. In fact, I am arguing that in the cultures of Afro-peoples there are characteristics that Afro-rhythms alone give rise to. These rhythms especially undergird and distinguish black music, which comprises the fundamental source of movement, momentum, and momentousness in black religious ritual. This religious ritual is in turn the location in which black peoples absorb African rhythms and concretize them in other aesthetic ways that *are* black culture.

Notes

1. Laura M. Townes, diary entry for April 28, 1862, Penn School Papers, Southern Historical Collection, University of North Carolina at Chapel Hill.
2. William Francis Allen, C. P. Ware, and L. M. Garrison, *Slave Songs of the United States* (New York: A. Simpson, 1867; Peter Smith, 1951), xiii–xiv.
3. John Paris, "The Moral and Religious Status of the African Race in the Southern States," Ms. 13, Southern Historical Collection, University of North Carolina at Chapel Hill.
4. Katrina Hazzard-Gordon, *Jookin': The Rise of Social Dance Formations in African-American Culture* (Philadelphia: Temple University Press, 1990), 14.
5. Ibid., 18, 77.
6. Ibid., 81–82.
7. Ibid., 67, 80.
8. Ibid., 93.
9. Ibid., 84.
10. Ibid., 19, 87.
11. Ibid., 87.
12. Ibid., 159.
13. Ibid., 87, 210.
14. Alain L. Locke, "The American Negro as Artist," *American Magazine of Art* 23 (September 1931), in Alain Locke, *The Critical Temper of Alain Locke: A Selection*

of His Essays on Art and Culture, ed. Jeffrey C. Stewart (New York: Garland, 1983), 171.

15. R. Nathaniel Dett, "Negro Music," in *The International Cyclopedia of Music and Musicians,* ed. Oscar Thompson (New York: Dodd, Mead, 1938); reprinted in Jon Michael Spencer, ed., *The R. Nathaniel Dett Reader: Essays on Black Sacred Music,* special issue of *Black Sacred Music: A Journal of Theomusicology* 5, no. 2 (Fall 1991): 127.

16. William Grant Still, "The Music of My Race," *Musica* 1, no. 5 (August 1941); translation in Jon Michael Spencer, ed., *The William Grant Still Reader: Essays on American Music,* special issue of *Black Sacred Music: A Journal of Theomusicology* 6, no. 2 (Fall 1992): 102.

17. Locke, "Youth Speaks," *Survey Graphic* 53, no. 11 (March 1925), in *The Critical Temper,* 14.

18. Locke, *The Negro and His Music* (Washington: Associates in Negro Folk Education, 1936), 139–40.

19. R. Nathaniel Dett, "From Bell Stand to Throne Room," *Etude* 52 (February 1934), in *The R. Nathaniel Dett Reader,* 97.

20. Still, "My Arkansas Boyhood"; Jon Michael Spencer, ed., in *The William Grant Still Reader,* 248.

21. Cited in Anne Key Simpson, *Follow Me: The Life and Music of R. Nathaniel Dett* (Metuchen, N.J.: Scarecrow, 1993), 333.

22. Locke to Charlotte Osgood Mason, March 12, 1936, Alain L. Locke Papers, Manuscripts Department, Moorland-Spingarn Research Center, Howard University.

23. W. E. B. Du Bois, *Dusk of Dawn: An Essay Toward an Autobiography of a Race Concept* (New York: Harcourt, Brace, 1940), 117.

24. Sterling Stuckey, *Slave Culture: Nationalist Theory and the Foundations of Black America* (New York: Oxford University Press, 1987), 17.

25. Victor Turner, *The Ritual Process: Structure and Antistructure* (Ithaca: Cornell University Press, 1969), 128.

26. Martin Buber, *I and Thou,* trans. Ronald Gregor Smith (Edinburgh: T & T Clark, 1937), 95, 100, 116.

27. Bruce Reed, *The Dynamics of Religion: Process and Movement in Christian Churches* (London: Darton, Longman and Todd, 1978), 15, 32, 34, 35.

28. Leonard E. Barrett, *Soul-Force: African Heritage in Afro-American Religion* (Garden City, N.Y.: Anchor/Doubleday, 1974), 10.

29. Leland Ferguson, *Uncommon Ground: Archaeology and Early African America, 1650–1800* (Washington, D.C.: Smithsonian Institution Press, 1992), 123.

30. Martin Luther King Jr., *Why We Can't Wait* (New York: Mentor, 1964), 61.

31. Carl E. Seashore, *Psychology of Music* (New York: McGraw-Hill, 1938), 142.

32. Ella Anderson Clark, "The Reminiscences of Ella Anderson Clark," Ms. 43, James Osgood Andrew Clark Papers, Special Collections Department, Emory University.

33. Howard Odum and Guy B. Johnson, *The Negro and His Songs* (Hatboro, Pa.: Folklore Associates, 1964), 34.

34. Walter Fauntroy, "The Social Action Mission of the Church," lecture at Duke University Divinity School, November 22, 1981.

35. Ferguson, *Uncommon Ground*, xliv.

36. Ibid., 120.

37. Ibid., 117.

38. Barrett, *Soul-Force*, 83–84.

Trickster on Trial

The Morality of
the Brer Rabbit Tales

William Courtland Johnson

As American historians undertake the belated process of writing the history of *all* the people, they have become increasingly aware that their traditional reliance on written "historical documents" has relatively little application to such nonliterate cultures as those of African American slaves and Native Americans. In the absence of such documents, in recent decades oral literature has been mined for its treasures. And while the scholarly use of such evidence has often proved richly rewarding and extremely revealing, it has also presented some exceptional interpretive challenges. One contemporary example of just such a challenge is reflected in the Brer Rabbit tales that are found in such abundance within the African American oral tradition. A trickster figure whose roots have been traced to western Africa, Brer Rabbit is a physically unimposing character who employs guile and cunning time and again to outwit and triumph over his more powerful opponents. That this fascinating and, at least to some observers, at times disquieting figure should hold such a ubiquitous presence within the folklore of an enslaved people is clearly a matter of no small consequence.

In addition to obvious questions over the precise origins of the tales, academic debate has been focused largely on the question of just how the relationship between Brer Rabbit and his enslaved creators should be interpreted. The most traditional, and certainly most straightforward, argument has been that these were intended as allegorical tales in which the black slave's identity was masked in the form of the Rabbit. This conclusion has not gone unchallenged, however, mainly because of the seeming amorality and brutality exhibited in a number of the tales. Nonetheless, those who have collected and transcribed the tales have, for the most part, expressed overwhelming support for the "Rabbit as slave" thesis. Joel Chandler Harris clearly communicated his agreement with such an interpretation when he observed that "it needs no scientific investigation to show why [the Negro] selects as his hero the weakest and most harmless of all animals. . . . It is not virtue that triumphs, but helplessness; it is not malice but mischievousness."[1] Abigail Christensen, writing in 1892, prefaced her volume of tales with the remark "It must be remembered that the Rabbit represents the colored man. He is not as large nor as strong, as swift . . . nor as handsome as the elephant, the alligator, the bear . . . but he is 'de mos' cunnin' man dat go on fo' leg'—and by this cunning he gains success."[2] And William J. Faulkner, whose tales were recalled from a boyhood relationship with a former slave, Simon Brown, concluded: "The slaves . . . perceived the rabbit as being, like themselves, an innocent victim pursued by larger, more powerful enemies."[3]

The "Rabbit as slave" interpretation has garnered considerable support from essayists and scholars as well. Novelist and social commentator Bernard Wolfe, in a 1949 article, attempted to reconcile what he viewed as Rabbit's apparent amorality with the "Rabbit as slave" interpretation by reminding its detractors of the harsh realities of the slave's world: "Like the slave, [the rabbit] has a supremely cynical view of the social world. . . . The world, in Brer Rabbit's wary eyes, is a jungle . . . a battle without rules." Robert Bone has emphasized this view even more forcefully, stating that the figure of Brer Rabbit "was forged in the crucible of slavery, and cannot be understood apart from the brutalities that gave it shape." And, most recently, John W. Roberts has stated: "When viewed within the reality faced by the creators of the tales, the moral and social justification for Brer Rabbit's duplicity in the literal situation pictured in many of the tales becomes clear."[4]

Still, a number of prominent folklorists have remained unconvinced or undecided as to whether the Rabbit is truly meant to symbolize the slave. Richard M. Dorson, for example, has equivocated on the issue: "Whether the rabbit represents an ego projection of the underdog Negro, who finds satisfaction in the little creature's discomfiture of the larger beasts and his breaking of cherished taboos imposed on the colored man . . . one cannot tell from the narrators." It is Dorson's contention that the figure of the slave character John is a much more accurate representation of the slave in Negro folklore.[5] Robert O'Meally has also expressed clear disagreement with those who would argue that the Rabbit and the slave are indeed one and the same: "[Brer Rabbit's] vanity, unscrupulousness, and greed for material and sexual prizes and sheer power make Rabbit seem closer to the powerful slave master than to the slave."[6]

Historians of slave culture have also lent their voices to the debate. Among the most notable and certainly most influential is Lawrence W. Levine, whose widely acclaimed 1977 work, *Black Culture and Black Con-*

sciousness, treats the slaves' trickster tales in such depth and complexity that a relatively detailed summary of his argument is called for. Levine asserts that the "Rabbit as slave" interpretation, while valid and legitimate to an extent, falls short of embracing "much of the complexity and ambiguity inherent in these tales."[7] He understands well the enduring appeal of such an association and concedes that in many instances "Brer Rabbit's victories became the victories of the slave."[8] But he also maintains that such a straightforward interpretation does not hold true for all of the tales and that the Rabbit tales, at times, have other meanings.

Thus, while Levine does not deny that the slave's life was often characterized by great harshness and evil, he insists that historians have tended to overlook the additional truth that slaveholders were also capable of "acts of kindness" and that their moral code was one emulated not only by their children, "but often by their slaves as well." As such, Levine maintains that while the "Rabbit as slave" interpretation is not without some validity, "once we relax the orthodoxy that the trickster and slave are necessarily one, other crucial levels of meaning and understanding are revealed." He finds that the Rabbit functioned on a number of allegorical levels: representing the slave within certain tales, the white master in others, and occasionally as a sort of universal irrational force. "The trickster served as agent of the world's irrationality and as reminder of man's fundamental helplessness. Whenever animals became too bloated with their power or importance or sense of control, the trickster was on hand to remind them of how things really were."[9] At bottom, while conceding that the tales provided a valuable form of psychological release for the slave, Levine contends that they did so in a much more open-ended and complex manner than is conveyed in the "Rabbit as slave" orthodoxy. To this end, he disagrees with Robert Bone's characterization of the slave's existence as one in which "all moral scruples [were] discarded in a fierce effort to survive,"[10] contending instead that the ethical universe of the slave was more ambiguous than most scholars have allowed, grounded in what he terms as "anarchic confusion."[11]

Levine supports this conclusion by arguing that many of the Brer Rabbit tales are morally incompatible with the "didactic" content permeating other expressions of slave folklore and spirituals, remarking that "in many respects the lessons embodied in the animal trickster tales ran directly counter to . . . the slaves' moralistic tales."[12] He finds that such important themes as friendship, family ties, humility, religious reverence, and parental obligations—themes clearly communicated within most forms of slave culture—are not only absent from the trickster tales but are often directly refuted by them.[13] Consequently, in many tales the Rabbit appears to be living in a "state of perpetual war" grounded in "hypocrisy and meaninglessness." And it is not simply Rabbit's opponents whose tactics reflect such amorality and brutality, but Rabbit as well. Given this, Levine judges the "Rabbit as slave" thesis an inadequate interpretive model for many of the tales.[14]

Levine's analysis of the slaves' trickster tales has influenced the writings of a number of other historians. Stanley Elkins, for example, in the most recent edition of his well-known work *Slavery: A Problem in American Institutional and Intellectual Life,* reinforces Levine's emphasis on Rabbit's alleged unscrupulousness and lack of respect for family and community, concluding that, at best, Rabbit is "one nasty little hustler."[15] Levine's conclusions are also reflected in historian and folklorist Charles Joyner's 1984 work, *Down by the Riverside: A South Carolina Slave Community.* And while Joyner's analysis is focused almost exclusively on slave tales gathered in a relatively small region of South Carolina, he nonetheless crafts an argument eerily reminiscent of Levine's, stating that "in tale after tale, despite his sly effectiveness, [the trickster] is a scoundrel who is always ready to cheat or deceive. His outstanding characteristic is his amorality, his complete disdain for either social or moral values."[16] Joyner's phrasing even tends to parrot Levine, asserting at one point that "duplicity and violence . . . are portrayed as everyday actions for the trickster."[17]

Importantly, however, Levine's interpretation of the tales is not unique. The emphasis he places on the amorality, violence, and unscrupulousness in many of the Brer Rabbit tales dovetails handily with nearly all other analyses from an array of disciplines, both prior to and since the publication of his work. But inasmuch as his analysis represents the most comprehensive and influential contemporary statement of what has long been the "consensus" view of the morality of the tales, it provides an inviting point of departure for critically assessing its validity. The goal of this essay is to clear away many of the misconceptions and outright falsehoods that have long clouded debate over the nature of the tales and to suggest an alternative path along which future research might proceed.

One finds that a key stumbling block in the argument of those who view Rabbit as amoral arises from their apparent reliance on peculiar or uncommon variants of familiar tales in support of larger generalizations. An illustration of this may be seen with respect to Levine's contention that Brer Rabbit was more than willing to include among the "panoply of his victims . . . the weak as well as the powerful." He illustrates this point by referring to a tale in which Mr. Man has trapped Brer Rabbit and secured him to a tree limb for safekeeping. Soon after, the Rabbit spies Brer Squirrel and convinces him that he is actually enjoying a cool swing in the breeze and would be willing to permit the Squirrel to take a turn. Unable to resist, the unassuming Squirrel takes the Rabbit's place—and ends up being cooked for Mr. Man's supper.[18] This is a variant of a tale that surfaces in many collections, but almost invariably involving a dupe that is, in actuality, a much stronger, more powerful opponent of Brer Rabbit's—such as Brer Wolf.[19] Thus, while Levine's generalization is indeed consistent with the tale he outlines, it is an extremely unusual variant, and a close reading of the hundreds of additional tales reveals no other instance of Brer Rabbit threatening the weak. To the contrary, one encounters instead a considerable number of tales that present Brer Rabbit as a friend—and even as the occasional victim[20]—of those smaller and weaker than himself.

An additional problem relates to the manner in which Levine recounts the details of a number of tales within his discussion—selectively highlighting some portions of the tales while at the same time conveniently omitting others. An example of such selective editing is reflected in his summary of a tale used in support of his contention that "in one tale after another the trickster proves to be as merciless as his stronger opponent."[21] He refers us here to a variant of the popular tale that has the Wolf chasing Brer Rabbit into a hollow log and then threatening to smoke him out. In this version, as in many others, Brer Rabbit escapes what would appear to be certain death by convincing the Wolf that there is a cache of honey inside the log. Once their positions are reversed, however, it is Brer Rabbit who proceeds to set fire to the Wolf. And while this tale is certainly not reflective of any willingness to "forgive and forget" or to "turn the other cheek" on the part of Brer Rabbit, Levine's presentation of the story neglects to mention the significant detail that it begins with the Wolf pursuing the Rabbit with every intention of eating him: "Haw! Budder, me got you now. You dodge me long time. Ebry man fuh isself."[22] Surely such an important element behind Brer Rabbit's behavior is highly relevant to any characterization of him as "merciless," but it is curiously absent from the analysis.

In yet another instance of questionable interpretation, Brer Rabbit is said to have "participated in the decapitation of Brer Raccoon," an action described as "an everyday occurrence for Rabbit . . . performed for no discernible motive."[23] The tale begins with Rabbit, Fox, and Raccoon in an alliance against Brer Lion. While attempting to take goods from Lion's bank, Raccoon becomes hopelessly ensnared in a trap. Concerned lest Brer Lion discover Raccoon in the trap and slay not only him but Raccoon's entire family, Rabbit and Fox "tek one swode an chop Buh Coon an bury eh an eh cloze, an leff Buh Coon nekked een de trap, so nobody kin tell who bin ketch."[24] Thus, in a manner significantly at odds with Levine's description, we find that Rabbit and Fox, knowing they were powerless to save Brer Raccoon, acted with sincere concern for the well-being of Raccoon's family.

On other occasions Levine's analysis not only tends to ignore significant details but actually distorts and mischaracterizes tales. For example, at one point he contends that Brer Rabbit is such a malicious and odious scoundrel that he is even willing to "cooly sacrifice his wife and little children in order to save himself from wolf's vengeance."[25] A close reading of the tale in question, however, renders this statement puzzling indeed. The story describes Brer Wolf smoking Brer Rabbit and his family out of their home in retribution for having been tricked out of a pail of fish. But Rabbit and his family manage to escape to the steep roof of their house, from which they are scarcely able to hang on in the thick, suffocating smoke. One by one Rabbit's wife and children, exhausted and overcome by the smoke, are forced to let go, despite Brer Rabbit's heart-wrenching pleas: "My chile you mus' hol' on. Aint you see dat man down dere gwine kill ou ef you drop down?" Rabbit watches helplessly as the Wolf catches and beheads each member of his family, and he barely escapes himself, badly injured by the Wolf, at tale's end.[26] Levine's interpretation is not only misleading but is challenged by evidence in tale after tale of Rabbit being extremely attentive to and protective of his family—providing them with food, arranging for their rescue when imperiled, or exacting revenge for any harm that comes to them.[27]

Then there is the overall selection of tales relative to Brer Rabbit's moral stance. In this context, Levine argues that "rarely are [the animals in the Brer Rabbit tales] caught performing acts of altruism," that Brer Rabbit is to be faulted for failing "to ask for help" from his fellow animals rather than steadfastly relying on deceit and cunning.[28] And yet within one of the most familiar collections of all—that of Joel Chandler Harris—we find Brer Rabbit, out for a walk, encountering the Wolf, who is painfully trapped under a rock. In an act of altruism, Rabbit moves the rock away only to be grabbed by the hungry Wolf. Rabbit then enlists the aid of Brer Terrapin and shrewdly convinces the Wolf that he should mediate their differences; luckily for Brer Rabbit, Brer Terrapin is wise to the Wolf and tricks him back under the rock.[29] So, in quite the obverse of the characterization of Brer Rabbit as an amoral scoundrel continually involved in acts of "senseless cruelty," we find Rabbit willing to perform selfless acts of kindness in the context of a harsh world where such actions are often repaid with treachery and deceit.

Numerous other instances of Brer Rabbit's willingness to act in concert with his fellow creatures may be found in Faulkner's collection, with "Who Got Brer Gilyard's Treasure?" representing but one example. Threatened by Brer Tiger and Brer Bear for refusing to divulge the secret means of getting at the treasure hidden in Brer Gilyard's cave, Rabbit finds himself in a desperate situation, tied up and imprisoned. Luckily, Brer Lizard comes to his aid, prompting Rabbit to exclaim, "Oh, Brer Lizard, the Lord must have sent you. He's always on the side of right. . . . And you can help me. First, I want you to get word to all the creatures to be down in front of Brer Gilyard's cave the way I told them, first thing in the morning." Brer Lizard does Rabbit's bidding, engaging the help of a "whole passle of other creatures" to carry out Rabbit's plan, and in the end they prevail not only over Brer Bear and Brer Tiger but over the evil Brer Gilyard as well.[30]

Rather than call attention to such altruism—and there are many such examples—Levine highlights a tale from Harris's collection in which Rabbit tricks Wolf's Granny into immersing herself in scalding water and then deceives Wolf into devouring her boiled remains.[31] He cites the tale as an example of the malicious Rabbit acting without provocation, although, once again, a reading of the tale shows Rabbit's actions to have been motivated not only by his longstanding and deadly rivalry with the predatory Brer Wolf but also by the Wolf's insulting—and ominous—failure to respond to Rabbit's friendly overtures: "Hi, B'er Wolf! wey you no fer mek answer wun me ahx you howdy? Wey fer you is do dis 'fo' me werry face? Wut mekky you do dis? . . . Come-a show you'se'f, B'er Wolf! Come-a show you'se'f. Be 'shame' fer not show you'se'f wun you' 'quaintun' come bisitin' wey you lif!"[32] Wolf's behavior not only angers Rabbit but alerts him to the possibility that it may be more than mere coincidence that Wolf's Granny is boiling water at the very moment of his arrival. Even Uncle Remus justifies Rabbit's action in the preface to the following tale, explaining it as a response to Wolf's earlier attempts to destroy him. And as for Wolf's Granny, "a wolf, even an old and feeble one, is still a wolf."[33]

Importantly, Levine also fails to distinguish between the impulses motivating Brer Rabbit and those of his predatory opponents, maintaining that "the slave could empathize with the tricked as well as the trickster." He argues in this vein, albeit unconvincingly, that the slave could "empathize" with the Wolf when he tricked the Rabbit into getting stuck to a tar baby as well as when he pretended he was dead in hopes of trapping Rabbit into coming to his funeral.[34] It seems oddly ironic that Levine focuses primarily on the Wolf in his analysis of Rabbit's opponents, for it is indeed the Wolf, more than any other predator, who consistently threatens Rabbit's existence. This deadly contest is recounted vividly in Harris's collection, and Christensen further develops it in a set of encounters between Rabbit and Wolf that finally conclude with Brer Rabbit acting in concert with Brer Whale to trap and kill Wolf, who is portrayed as synonymous with greed: "All de people da mek dance in da road an' laugh at

Br'er Wolf, an' tell 'e chilluns, 'Greedy kill you daddy, an' ef [you all] don'
tek care, greedy da kill you.' '"[35] Faulkner's collection progresses similarly,
with tale after tale depicting the evil Wolf scheming against Brer Rabbit—
and, at times, even against Rabbit's children.[36]

In fact, in nearly every collection of Brer Rabbit tales one witnesses
Wolf's willingness to engage in such gruesome and heinous acts as selling
his grandparents[37] or decapitating Rabbit's family over a pail of fish. An
evil-minded trickster, Wolf is more powerful than the Rabbit and committed to his destruction. Left with little choice, Brer Rabbit does not hesi-
tate to employ trickery, deceit, and violence to prevail over his mortal
enemy. The distinction that Levine fails to detect is that Rabbit's actions
are consistently governed by well-defined limits with respect to his family
and others who pose no danger to him. In this respect, his characterization
of Brer Rabbit's actions as being as merciless and morally reprehensible
as those of Brer Wolf is ill considered.

This brings us to the nettlesome issue of whether greater validity can
be assigned to particular tales or sets of tales over others: is one variation
of a tale, whatever its origin or history, as legitimate and revealing as any
other? It is a complex problem, for a number of factors come into play in
making such a determination. There can be little question, however, that
among the most important of these is knowledge both of the specific origin of a tale as well as the actual context in which it has been related and
transcribed. In this connection, a paramount consideration in determining
the degree of veracity in slave tales is the well-known and understandable
refusal of blacks to reveal their innermost thoughts and beliefs to
whites—a matter of tremendous consequence when dealing with issues
of faith and morality, especially under slavery and segregation. With respect to the Brer Rabbit tales, one notes with considerable interest that
Harris, a white Southerner, did not literally transcribe the stories he was
told but instead sketched out plot outlines briefly while in the field and
only later fleshed out the details.[38] In contrast to Harris, Northerner Abigail Christensen took fewer liberties in practicing her craft, prefacing her
collection with the assurance that its contents are "comprised of verbatim
reports from numerous sable story-tellers of the Sea Islands."[39] And, as
previously mentioned, black folklorist William J. Faulkner's tales are recalled from a warm childhood relationship with a former Virginia slave,
Simon Brown. Thus, while other factors certainly need to be considered
in making a judgment about Rabbit's moral stance, it is evident that not
all tales or collections of tales carry equal weight.

Given this, it seems revealing indeed that Brer Rabbit as presented
in Christensen's collection bears almost no resemblance to the menacing
figure portrayed by so many scholars. This is not to suggest that the Brer

Rabbit in her tales is not a trickster—with all that that implies—but only that he is hardly unknown for acts of kindness and even heroism, seeking to provide food for the hungry forest animals in "De Rabbit, De Bear, 'An De Locus Tree" and even kindly showing the Wolf how to gather eggs in "De Wolf, De Rabbit 'an De Whale's Eggs."[40] And while it is true that Christensen's Rabbit engages in acts of mischief and cunning, he consistently does so with justification: the need for food or water, in response to an imminent threat, or as a means of neutralizing his sworn enemies. Nowhere in this collection does one find a basis for the portrait of Brer Rabbit as an unscrupulous rascal engaging in slavery,[41] preying upon smaller creatures, sacrificing his own family, or otherwise behaving in a manner inconsistent with survival in a harsh and unforgiving world.

And once again, in Faulkner's important collection, one finds an array of very familiar tale variants that challenge scholarly characterizations of the tales as "amoral."[42] One encounters in this body of tales, to an even more pronounced extent than in Christensen's, a trickster hero who acts craftily and assertively on behalf of his interests while remaining protective of his family, sensitive to the needs of the weak, and guided by a sense of justice and morality. In fact, there is not a single instance in this collection where one finds support for a description of "amorality" or "hypocrisy and meaninglessness" in the Brer Rabbit tales. To Faulkner, the tales symbolize the struggle between good and evil, in which Brer Rabbit's "antagonists were wicked, on the side of the Devil. As the slaves identified with the Rabbit, they felt themselves to be allied with God, and their white adversaries to be henchmen of the Devil."[43] Such an interpretation is clearly at odds with the characterization of most scholars and, perhaps most importantly, wholly in keeping with other expressions of slave folklore such as slave songs, especially spirituals.[44]

Faulkner's body of tales also argues against the thesis that in American slavery "divine trickster figures disappeared."[45] For one finds in Faulkner's collection a Rabbit trickster of immaculate ethical bearing who acts decisively and heroically on the side of "right."[46] This is reflective not only of Christianity's impact on the slave community but of the enduring influence of the divine trickster figures of the West African oral tradition as well, such as Anansi the spider or Legba, messenger of the gods, who often intervened between men and the gods to alter men's destinies within a world ostensibly governed by Fate and predestination.[47] Faulkner's Rabbit fulfills such a function in a number of tales, employing his considerable powers of cleverness and vigilance to achieve goals inspired by much more than merely secular needs.[48] This role is expressed most transparently at the conclusion of "The Tiger and the Big Wind," as Brer Rabbit subdues the evil Tiger and urges his fellow animals to partake of the Lord's bounty: "And you children, gather up your crocus sacks and water buckets. Get all the pears and drinking water you want, because the Good Lord doesn't love a stingy man. He put the food and water here for all His creatures to enjoy."[49] And, once again, in "Brer Rabbit Rescues His Children," we find Rabbit, "heart pound[ing] with fear," acting bravely and assertively not only to thwart great evil but to save his five beloved children from certain death as well.[50] Clearly, the heroic spiritual leader portrayed in Faulkner's tales bears little resemblance to the sinister trickster characterized by others.

Of course, the primary impulse informing scholarly questioning of the "Rabbit as slave" interpretation is the perceived inconsistency between the tales and the moral posture of the slaves as articulated in a variety of other cultural expressions, especially spirituals. In fact, the comparison between the trickster tales and spirituals strikes at the heart of the Brer Rabbit debate because, at bottom, the controversy has its wellsprings in the inability of a number of scholars to reconcile what they perceive as Rabbit's gratuitously violent and vengeful behavior with Christian doctrines of forgiveness and love. Most students of slave culture are in accord with the thesis that the vast majority of slaves were "converted to a religion which stressed their humanity and even their divinity" and that "there can be no question that a substantial number of slaves sincerely believed in the values of the religion they embraced and in part refashioned." And it is for this reason, more than any other, that a number of scholars reject the notion that "slaves completely identified with their animal trickster hero."[51]

However, the thesis that a majority of slaves fully embraced Christianity presents, to say the least, some difficulties, given the implicit suggestion that slaves somehow identified with their white enslavers. In fact, in recent years growing numbers of scholars have pointed to evidence suggesting that fewer than twenty percent of Negro slaves had formally converted to the white man's religion by the time of the Civil War.[52] And while these findings have generated considerable debate, the question of the actual extent of slave exposure to and acceptance of Christian teaching clearly calls for further research and reflection.[53] Despite such controversy, however, it is also apparent that African religious traditions, richly expressed in song and dance as well as in the tales, continued to shape and influence the slaves' moral and spiritual universe throughout the antebellum period.

With respect to dance, the continued presence of African spiritual influences is most evident in the widespread observance of the sacred ring shout, described by one former slave as a time in which "de black folks get off in de bottom and shouts and sings and prays. Dey get in de ring dance. It am just a kind of shuffle, den it get faster and faster and dey gets warmed up and moans and shouts and claps and dances. . . . Sometimes dey sings and shouts all night."[54] The enduring vitality of this African ritual even to slaves influenced by Christianity is reflected most strongly in its clear association with religious awakening and conversion. AME Bishop Daniel Payne, who strongly objected to the dance as a "heathen-ish" rite, learned firsthand of this relationship at a spiritual gathering of freedmen in Pennsylvania, where it was explained to him that "at camp-meeting there must be a ring here, a ring there, a ring over yonder, or sinners will not get converted."[55]

The symbolic importance of the ring or circle in Negro spiritual ex-pression is underscored in European traveler Fredrika Bremer's account of an interracial evangelical camp meeting near Charleston, South Caro-lina in 1850, where she witnessed among slaves, mostly from South Caro-lina, *circles* of women dancing "the holy dance" for the newly converted; *circles* of people holding hands, rocking and singing joyously; and even a "vast" *circle* of tents "of all imaginable forms and colours."[56] As explained by Africanist Robert Farris Thompson, in the African sacred tradition the circle represents the "ideal balancing of the vitality of the world of the living with the visionaries of the world of the dead," reflective of a "circu-lar movement of human souls."[57] The continued observance of the ring shout ritual throughout the slave community, especially among those "converted" to Christianity, demonstrates beyond question the tenacious power and influence of the slaves' African cultural inheritance.

While ring shout participants in the antebellum period were permit-ted a measure of personal expressiveness, there were also rigidly enforced rules. Folklorist Harold Courlander notes that "the tension generated in the course of the shout has certain approved outlets, such as ecstatic sei-zures or possessions, but the feet are required to be kept under control. A person who violates this commonly understood proscription by crossing his feet—that is to say, by dancing—is admonished or evicted from the service."[58] It is noteworthy as well that such structure and order were maintained even during the frenzy of possession, as Frederika Bremer concluded from her study of Negro religious observance in the South in the 1850s: "Under possession the worshipper . . . merges his identity in that of the god, losing control of his conscious faculties and knowing noth-ing of what he does until he comes to himself. This phenomenon, the outstanding manifestation of West African religion, is, for all its hysterical quality, by no means undisciplined."[59] In light of such evidence, charges that the slaves' world was almost overwhelmingly "irrational" or "chaotic" are called into question.

African influences shaped the slaves' songs as well, especially the spirituals, which were often composed and performed within the context of the ring shout. This complex yet profoundly revealing association is described vividly in writer and folklorist James Weldon Johnson's boyhood recollection of religious worship:

> The music, starting, perhaps, with a Spiritual becomes a wild, monotonous chant. The same musical phrase is repeated over and over one, two, three, four, five hours. The words become a repetition of an incoherent cry. The very monotony of sound and motion produces an ecstatic state. Women, screaming, fall to the ground prone and quivering. Men, exhausted, drop out of the shout. But the ring closes up and moves around and around.[60]

Civil War leader Thomas Wentworth Higginson also describes in rich detail Negro soldiers singing Christian lyrics while dancing in the counterclockwise movement of the ring, with its "ceaseless drumming and clapping, in perfect cadence."[61] The relationship between African and Christian spiritual influences is also made clear in an 1867 article on Negro religious observance in the New York *Nation:* "Sometimes they dance silently, sometimes as they shuffle they sing the chorus of the spiritual, and sometimes the song itself is also sung by the dancers."[62] It is also significant that the very structure and pattern of the songs bear unmistakable African imprints, particularly with respect to their incremental leading lines and choral iteration.[63] And thus it is through this subtle yet hypnotic confluence of Christianity and African spirituality that a more complex sacred tradition than scholars have led us to believe germinated and flowered in slavery's bitter soil.[64]

The inextricable relationship between the slaves' sacred worldview and the trickster tales is rendered powerfully—and symbolically—in the tale "Bur Rabbit in Red Hill Churchyard," from South Carolina collector E. C. L. Adams's brilliant collection, *Tales of the Congaree.* Being watched surreptitiously one moonlit night in a graveyard, Brer Rabbit is described "settin' on top of a grave playin' a fiddle," with "all kind er little beasts ... runnin' 'round." Then, after a few moments, "Bur Rabbit stop playin', put he fiddle under he arm an' step off de grave. He walk off a little piece an' guin some sort er sign to de little birds an' beasts, an' dey form dey self into a *circle* 'round de grave. An' dat was when I knowed sump'n strange was guh happen." Brer Rabbit then resumed fiddling, and "Bur Mockin' Bird jine him an' whistle a chune dat would er made de angels weep." After stopping once more, Brer Rabbit bowed, and then, amazingly, "de snow on de grave crack an' rise up, an' de grave open an' I see Simon rise up out er dat grave."[65]

Thus, in a manner not unlike that of the sacred tricksters Anansi and Legba, Rabbit assumes in Red Hill Churchyard the role of an African priest, intervening between mortal beings and the ineffable forces of the universe, navigating with considerable skill the interstices between the natural and supernatural.[66] The vivid descriptions in the tale of the complex linkage of music, circular dance, and communication beyond the boundaries of this world recall slave narrative accounts of antebellum funeral ceremonies, such as one from St. Simons Island, Georgia: "Dey go in a long pruhcession tuh duh burying ground an dey beat duh drums long duh way an dey submit duh body tuh duh ground. Den dey dance roun in a ring an dey motion wid duh hans. Dey sing duh body tuh duh grabe an den dey let it down an dey succle roun in duh dance."[67] Clearly, Brer Rabbit's participation as religious leader in this most sacred of all ceremonies establishes his prominent position within the slaves' spiritual tradition.

Anthropologist Melville Herskovits has reflected on a particularly revealing aspect of the slaves' West African religious legacy: "The African . . . recognizes the fact that in reality there is no absolute good and no absolute evil, [and] that nothing can exert an influence for good without at the very least causing inconvenience elsewhere; that nothing is so evil that it cannot be found to have worked benefit to someone." Herskovits also refers to a pronounced willingness among Africans to incorporate the gods of others—particularly those of politically and militarily powerful tribes—into one's own belief system.[68] This willingness to appropriate religious values from others without abandoning one's own undoubtedly continued among African descendants in America. Students of slave culture, such as W. E. B. DuBois, have long commented on this hybridization or intermixture of profoundly differing spiritual traditions, observing that the converted slave, confronting in the peculiar institution "the sum of all villainies, the cause of all sorrow, the root of all prejudice," tended to reshape and redefine Christianity to meet his unique spiritual requirements, his religion becoming "darker and more intense, and into his ethics crept a note of revenge, into his songs a day of reckoning close at hand. The 'Coming of the Lord' swept this side of Death, and came to be a thing to be hoped for in this day."[69]

In this respect, one allows that "Christian" slave morality was governed not only by New Testament strictures promoting love, forgiveness, and the promise of ultimate salvation, but by a consciousness of the Christian God's uncompromising justice in this world as well. The validity of this interpretation is reflected in the admonitions of the antebellum black Christian leader David Walker:

The man who would not fight under our Lord and Master Jesus Christ, in the glorious and heavenly cause of freedom and of God—to be delivered from the most wretched, abject and sterile slavery, that ever a people was afflicted with since the foundation of the world, to the present day—ought to be kept with all his children or family, in slavery, or in chains, to be butchered by his cruel enemies.[70]

Walker's appeal for deliberate and retributive action in this world—a theme of considerable importance in the Brer Rabbit tales—is echoed by Frederick Douglass, also a devout Christian:

The slaveholder, kind or cruel, is a slaveholder still—the every hour violator of the just and inalienable rights of man; and he is, therefore, every hour silently whetting the knife of vengeance for his own throat. He never lisps a syllable in commendation of the fathers of this republic, nor denounces any attempted oppression of himself, without inviting the knife to his own throat, and asserting the rights of rebellion for his own slaves.[71]

In light of such evidence, it is lamentable indeed that scholars have focused to such an inordinate degree on the "irrationality and amorality" of the Brer Rabbit tales. For once assessed within the context of enduring African cultural and spiritual traditions and Christian conversion, the argument that the tales fail to reflect the moral universe of the slaves rings hollow.

Notes

1. Joel Chandler Harris, *The Complete Tales of Uncle Remus* (Boston: Houghton Mifflin, 1955), xxv. Harris fudges on whether or not the tales were truly allegorical, however, stating, "It seems to me to be to a certain extent allegorical, albeit such an interpretation may be unreasonable."
2. A. M. H. Christensen, *Afro-American Folklore* (Boston: J. G. Cupples, 1892; reprint ed., New York: Negro Universities Press, 1969), xi.
3. William J. Faulkner, *The Days When the Animals Talked: Black American Folktales and How They Came to Be* (Chicago: Follet, 1977), 6.
4. Bernard Wolfe, "Uncle Remus and the Malevolent Rabbit: 'Takes a Limber-Toe Gemmun fer ter Jump Jim Crow'," in R. Bruce Bickley Jr., ed., *Critical Essays on Joel Chandler Harris* (Boston: G. K. Hall, 1981), 74–75; Robert Bone, "The Oral Tradition," in Bickley, *Critical Essays*, 134; John W. Roberts, *From*

Trickster to Badman: The Black Folk Hero in Slavery and Freedom (Philadelphia: University of Pennsylvania Press, 1989), 37.

5. Richard M. Dorson, *American Negro Folktales* (Greenwich, Conn.: Fawcett, 1967), 66, 124.

6. E. C. L. Adams, *Tales of the Congaree*, with an introduction by Robert G. O'Meally (Chapel Hill: University of North Carolina Press, 1987), lvii.

7. Lawrence Levine, *Black Culture and Black Consciousness: Afro-American Folk Thought from Slavery to Freedom* (New York: Oxford University Press, 1977), 114.

8. Ibid., 113.

9. Ibid., 114, 118, 120–21, 115–16.

10. Bone, "The Oral Tradition," 138.

11. Levine, *Black Culture*, 113.

12. Ibid., 115–16.

13. Ibid., 91–97.

14. Ibid., 116, 114.

15. Stanley Elkins, *Slavery: A Problem in American Institutional and Intellectual Life* (Chicago: University of Chicago Press, 1976), 282–83. It is significant to point out, given the larger body of Elkins's and Levine's work, that this is one of the very few points of agreement that one detects between them. Richard Dorson, in his review of Levine's work, also echoes Elkins in questioning whether the slaves identified with Brer Rabbit to even a limited extent, "since if the slaves had a slave trickster, John, to represent them directly, why did they need an animal?" (review of *Black Culture and Black Consciousness*, in *Journal of American Folklore* 93 [April 1980], 187–89).

16. Charles Joyner, *Down by the Riverside: A South Carolina Slave Community* (Urbana: University of Illinois Press, 1984), 177.

17. Ibid., 179. Compare to Levine's statement in *Black Culture* that "acts of senseless cruelty . . . are an everyday occurrence for Rabbit" (117).

18. Levine, *Black Culture*, 108.

19. See Charles C. Jones, *Negro Myths from the Georgia Coast, Told in the Vernacular* (Columbia, S.C.: State Company, 1925), 140–43. This tale type is also examined in some detail in Florence E. Baer, *Sources and Analogues of the Uncle Remus Tales*, Publication of FF Communications, ed. Prof. Dr. Lauri Honko, no. 228 (Helsinki: Academia Scientiarum Fennica, 1980), 48–49; also in Dorson, *American Negro Folktales*, 83–86.

20. Levine's own discussion offers support for this point, citing two separate tales in which Rabbit falls victim to the trickery of Partridge and Frog; see *Black Culture*, 110. Also see Joyner's discussion of this issue in which he observes that "Buh Rabbit rarely meets his match," but "when he does, it is at the hands of even smaller, weaker creatures" (178).

21. Levine, *Black Culture*, 107.

22. Jones, *Negro Myths*, 108–10. Also see an important variant of this tale in Faulkner, *Days When the Animals Talked*, 139–40, which begins with Brer Wolf jumping out from behind some bushes and pursuing the surprised Rabbit, crying: "I'm a gonna eat you this time for sure."

23. Levine, *Black Culture*, 117. It should be noted that this is also a most unusual tale for which no variant type was found in the folklore literature.

24. Jones, *Negro Myths*, 82–83. The dialect in this passage might be translated as follows: Rabbit and Fox took a sword and chopped [decapitated] Brer Racoon, burying him [his head] and his clothes, and left Brer Racoon naked in the trap, so no one can tell who's been caught.

25. Levine, *Black Culture*, 117.

26. Christensen, *Afro-American Folklore*, 26–35.

27. Ibid., 108–16; Jones, *Negro Myths*, 102–4; Faulkner, *Days When the Animals Talked*, 168–77; Baer, *Sources and Analogues*, 40–41. Levine himself provides a tale supporting this point, but in a different context: Rabbit and Wolf agree to sell each other's grandparents in order to buy butter. Rabbit arranges for his grandparents to escape, however, and only the Wolf's are actually sold. The Rabbit, of course, ends up with all the butter as well. Levine points to the tale as an illustration of Rabbit's sly, tricky ways, but it might also be seen as a reflection of his concern for the well-being of his family. Had Rabbit truly been as scurrilous as Levine describes, both sets of grandparents would have been sold in order to purchase an even greater quantity of butter! See Levine, *Black Culture*, 109; and Christensen, *Afro-American Folklore*, 73–80.

28. Levine, *Black Culture*, 116.

29. Harris, *The Complete Tales of Uncle Remus*, 315–19.

30. Faulkner, *Days When the Animals Talked*, 180–81.

31. Levine, *Black Culture*, 117.

32. Harris, *The Complete Tales of Uncle Remus*, 315–16. The unfamiliar dialect in this passage might be translated as "Hi, Brer Wolf! Why don't you answer me when I greet you? Why do you insult me in such a fashion? What makes you do this? Come show yourself, Brer Wolf! Come show yourself! It would be a shame for you not to show yourself when an acquaintance comes to visit where you live!"

33. See Wayne Mixon, "The Ultimate Irrelevance of Race: Joel Chandler Harris and Uncle Remus in Their Time," *Journal of Southern History* 56 (August 1990): 473.

34. Levine, *Black Culture*, 119.

35. Christensen, *Afro-American Folklore*, 116.

36. Faulkner, *Days When the Animals Talked*, 168–77.

37. Ibid., n. 27.

38. Dorson, *American Negro Folktales*, 14.

39. Christensen, *Afro-American Folktales*, xii–xiii.

40. Ibid., 23–25, 108–16.

41. Levine makes this charge in the context of his discussion of the amoral nature of the tales, stating that the animals "mouthed lofty platitudes and professed belief in noble ideals but spent much of their time manipulating, oppressing, *enslaving* one another. They surrounded themselves with meaningless etiquette, encased themselves in rigid hierarchies, dispensed rewards not to the most deserving but to the most crafty and least scrupulous." Curiously, he

provides no evidence in support of this contention, nor has a careful reading of his primary sources revealed any basis for it (118; italics added).

42. See especially "The Tiger and the Big Wind," 89–94; "Brer Rabbit Rescues His Children," 168–77; and "Who Got Brer Gilyard's Treasure," 178–84.

43. Faulkner, *Days When the Animals Talked*, 6.

44. The argument that the slaves' trickster tales are inconsistent with other forms of folklore has enjoyed considerable influence, most notably in the work of Stanley Elkins, who writes: "The case for 'community' [in slave folklore] holds up very well throughout the entire discussion of music, and is especially persuasive with regard to the spirituals. But with the folk-tales the claim is dropped; there, with entirely different forces at work, it somehow does not apply at all." See Elkins, *Slavery*, 282. It is also instructive to point out that celebrated novelist Toni Morrison's *Tar Baby* (New York: Alfred A. Knopf, 1981), based loosely on the well-known Brer Rabbit tale, has as its central character a most resolute and resourceful black man named Son who reflects qualities highly reminiscent of Faulkner's Rabbit: devoted to family and community; considerate and helpful to those less fortunate; admired by those who know him, especially the ladies; and always prepared to act vigorously and decisively, at times even extralegally, when confronted with issues of racial injustice or personal survival. And although Morrison provides no explicit insight into the sources for her interpretation, it seems evident that she simply read the tales.

45. Levine, *Black Culture*, 105.

46. Faulkner, *Days When the Animals Talked*, 185. This term is employed at the close of Faulkner's final tale when, after Brer Rabbit has thwarted the evil schemes of Brer Gilyard, Brer Tiger, and Brer Bear on behalf of the weaker denizens of the forest, Faulkner states: "And that was the end of all the troubles that Brer Rabbit and his friends had with Brer Gilyard and the other bad creatures in the Pee Dee River Swamp. Once and for all Brer Rabbit had won out because he had *right* on his side."

47. George P. Rawick, *From Sundown to Sunup: The Making of the Black Community* (Westport, Conn.: Greenwood Press, 1972), 98–100. For a fuller discussion of African tricksters and their sacred function see Melville J. Herskovits, *Myth of the Negro Past* (New York: Harper and Brothers, 1941), 71.

48. Faulkner, *Days When the Animals Talked*, 6.

49. Ibid., 94. In light of the substance of the debate over Rabbit's identity, Faulkner not only marshals powerful support in favor of the thesis that Rabbit represents the slave, but the reasons he offers for doing so differ in significant ways from those expressed by other scholars and tale collectors. For among those voicing support for the "Rabbit as slave" thesis, most conclude that, despite Rabbit's apparent unscrupulousness and amorality, the slaves were still able to identify with him because, as Robert Bone maintains, Brer Rabbit "was forged in the crucible of slavery." Faulkner rejects such reasoning, insisting that slavery, while indeed unjust, did not therefore create among its victims a justification for amorality or unscrupulousness. To the contrary, the slaves,

like Brer Rabbit, resisted injustice with impressive cunning and fortitude but consistently within well-defined boundaries, mindful of their ultimate responsibility to family, community, and their moral and spiritual inheritance. Faulkner thus concludes that "through Brer Rabbit and the tales of his daring, enslaved blacks were able to see themselves not only as morally superior to their white masters, but as ultimately triumphant over them" (*Days When the Animals Talked*, 6).

50. Ibid., 174.

51. Forrest G. Wood has been among the leaders of those challenging the consensus interpretation. He even questions the sincerity of those who did adopt Christianity: "to what extent the slave's conversion was a consequence of his bondage, as a convenient escape mechanism or a genuine spiritual commitment, is a question that has never been—and probably never can be—fully answered." See Wood, *The Arrogance of Faith: Christianity and Race in America From the Colonial Era to the Twentieth Century* (New York: Alfred A. Knopf, 1990): 138, 149.

52. The extent of Christian conversion among slaves is controversial; works that challenge the thesis of mass conversion include Wood, *The Arrogance of Faith;* Sterling Stuckey, *Slave Culture: Nationalist Theory and the Foundations of Black America* (New York: Oxford University Press, 1987); Eileen Southern, *The Music of Black Americans: A History,* 2nd ed. (New York: W. W. Norton, 1983); and Leslie Howard Owens, *This Species of Property: Slave Life and Culture in the Old South* (New York: Oxford University Press, 1977). Among the many mainstream works arguing in favor of mass conversion are Eugene Genovese, *Roll, Jordan, Roll: The World the Slaves Made* (New York: Random House, 1974); John Blassingame, *The Slave Community: Plantation Life in the Antebellum South* (New York: Oxford University Press, 1979); John B. Boles, *Black Southerners, 1619–1869* (Lexington, Ky.: University Press of Kentucky, 1983); and, perhaps most comprehensively, Albert J. Raboteau, *Slave Religion: The "Invisible Institution" in the Antebellum South* (New York: Oxford University Press, 1978). Raboteau, like a number of historians of slave religion, expresses awareness of the shortcomings of the "mission to the slaves" and the fact that church membership figures in the 1850s reflect fewer than half a million formal slave converts. And yet his overall discussion tends to ignore such factors and maintains, with little evidence, that a majority of slaves were indeed converted, stating that "not all slaves were Christian, nor were all those who accepted Christianity members of a church, but the doctrines, symbols, and vision of life preached by Christianity were familiar to most" (176–212).

54. Silvia King, in Norman R. Yetman, ed., *Life Under the Peculiar Institution: Selections from the Slave Narrative Collection* (New York: Holt, Rinehart, and Winston, 1970), 200.

55. Daniel Payne, *The Recollections of Seventy Years* (New York: Arno Press and New York *Times,* 1968; originally published 1888), 92, 255–56. For a detailed analysis of the ring shout and the manner in which slaves adapted it to Christian worship, see Mechal Sobel, *Trabelin' On: The Slave Journey to an Afro-Baptist Faith* (Westport, Conn.: Greenwood Press, 1979).

56. Fredrika Bremer, *Homes of the New World,* Vol. 1 (New York: Harper and Brothers, 1857), 318–19.

57. Robert Farris Thompson, *Flash of the Spirit: African and Afro-American Art and Philosophy* (New York: Random House, 1983), 106.

58. Harold Courlander, *A Treasury of African Folklore* (New York: Marlowe and Co., 1995), 366.

59. Fredrika Bremer, *Caste and Class in a Southern Town* (New York, 1850), 6.

60. James Weldon Johnson, ed., *The Book of American Negro Spirituals* (New York: The Viking Press, 1925), 33.

61. Thomas Wentworth Higginson, *Army Life in a Black Regiment* (Williamstown, Mass.: Corner House Publishers, 1984; originally published 1870), 17.

62. Quoted in Courlander, *Treasury of Afro-American Folklore,* 365.

63. Johnson, *American Negro Spirituals,* 23; Raboteau, *Slave Religion,* 70.

64. Courlander points out that the marriage of Christian and African spiritual expressions was not accomplished easily, describing the ring shout as "a fusion of two seemingly irreconcilable attitudes toward religious behavior. In most of Africa, dance, like singing and drumming, is an integral part of supplication. . . . In the Euro-Christian tradition, however, dancing in church is generally regarded as a profane act. The ring shout in the United States provides a scheme which reconciles both principles. The circular movement, shuffling steps, and stamping conform to African traditions of supplication, while by definition this activity is not recognized as a 'dance.' " Courlander, joining a number of other scholars, suggests in this vein that slaves modified the ring shout by eliminating the crossing of feet in order to overcome white objections to dancing. To this date, however, no evidence has been presented demonstrating that the crossing of legs was ever a part of the ring shout; see *Treasury of Afro-American Folklore,* 366. Like their religion, the slaves' folklore also cannot be understood without sensitivity to their African cultural inheritance. In this respect, literary critic and novelist Michael Thelwell reminds us that in Africa, the tales "were not told so much as performed, dramatically reenacted, so that the accomplished taleteller had to be master of a range of skills. He was at once actor, mime, impressionist, singer, dancer, composer, and conductor, using his range of artistic skills and even the audience and environment to create a multidimensional experience that has no obvious equivalent in Western culture." Folklorist William J. Faulkner, having committed to memory the exact manner in which tales were related to him by former slave Simon Brown, has left extant recordings that provide unmistakable evidence of Simon's skill in most of these areas. See Thelwell, *Duties, Pleasures, and Conflicts: Essays in Struggle* (Amherst, Mass.: University of Massachusetts Press, 1987), 212.

65. Adams, *Tales of the Congaree,* 235–36.

66. See Rawick, *From Sundown to Sunup,* 98. Rawick detects a clear continuity between Brer Rabbit in the New World and the sacred African tricksters, such as Legba, "the trickster messenger of the gods. In these West African versions there is a sense of organic relationship between the people and Legba . . . and

the rest of the forces of the universe. The distance between the natural and the supernatural is not felt, but Legba or Anansi are clearly not totally of the sphere of men, although they certainly are in crucial ways like humans."

67. WPA Georgia Writers' Program, *Drums and Shadows: Survival Studies among the Georgia Coastal Negroes* (Athens, Ga.: University of Georgia Press, 1940), 180.

68. Melville J. Herskovits, *The Myth of the Negro Past* (New York: Harper and Brothers, 1941), 73–74, 72.

69. W. E. B. DuBois, *The Souls of Black Folk* (New York: Alfred A. Knopf, 1993; originally published in 1903), 7, 163.

70. David Walker, "Walker's Appeal," in Sterling Stuckley, ed., *The Ideological Origins of Black Nationalism* (Boston: Beacon Press, 1972), 51.

71. Frederick Douglass, *My Bondage and My Freedom* (New York: Miller, Orton and Mulligan, 1855; Arno Press and New York Times, 1969), 268–69. The African-Christian moral universe characterized so vividly by Walker and Douglass underscores well why the Faulkner collection in particular is of such significance to our understanding of the Brer Rabbit tales, for hand in hand with the Christian themes articulated throughout Faulkner's tales, one also finds Rabbit unhesitant in allowing a pack of hounds to attack Brer Fox, unremorseful in depriving Brer Wolf of his share of a crop they were growing together, and boastful in engineering the singeing of Brer Gator to make a point. Yet in a manner consistent with Walker's and Douglass's interpretations, Faulkner's Rabbit also makes clear his purpose and rational justification for such acts.

Motherwit
in Southern Religion
A Womanist Perspective

Jacqueline D. Carr-Hamilton

This essay emerged in response to several questions. First, what is "motherwit," and how is it challenged by womanist God-talk?[1] Further, how are motherwit and womanist God-talk connected with southern religion? Last, there is the question of the universalization of the motherwit spirit within the African American community and experience.

Motherwit is the collective body of female wisdom—both formal and informal, oral and written, spiritual and social—passed on from generation to generation by African American females. It is a force rooted in the cultural and religious traditions of African American women, but it transcends the barriers of any set of social or religious principles. It is instead the strength of the total experience of black females, which has helped them survive their diaspora experience in the Western World. The presence of motherwit in the New World, however, cannot be understood apart from the legacy of this tradition among African women from nationalities such as the Yoruba, Mende, BaKongo, and other peoples of African descent. In this tradition, motherwit is matrifocal (mother and grandmother–focused); it is a pan-Africanist spirit binding women of African ancestry together in a way that they are not linked to other peoples.

Womanist theology, or God-talk, as described below by Delores S. Williams, is an excellent example of the essence of motherwit. She says:

> Like Hagar's story, African-American women's story has been closely associated with motherhood. Sociologists La-Frances Rodgers Rose and Joyce Landau claim that the social and economic significance of motherhood in Africa did not lose its importance when African women were brought to America and enslaved. The close bond between black women and children that existed in Africa was reinforced in the slaveocracy. . . . All of this African-derived female

knowledge was useful in the slaveocracy. Slave women could nurse and nurture their own children and also "mammy" the slave master's children.[2]

This African-derived female wisdom and knowledge provide the spiritual underpinning for African American folk religion, which is central to the motherwit spirit. As indicated originally by Melville Jean Herskovits in *The Myth of the Negro Past,* African retentions in the United States, especially in areas like Louisiana, Florida, Virginia, and the Gullah territory of South Carolina, are abundantly present.[3] Robert Farris Thompson, Joseph E. Holloway, Mechal Sobel, and others have demonstrated how Africanisms such as motherwit have survived.[4] Even E. Franklin Frazier, who disputed Herskovits, had to acknowledge the "Negro grandmother's importance . . . as granny or midwife . . . as the repository of folk wisdom concerning the inscrutable ways of nature."[5] Notwithstanding these facts, we should hasten to note that motherwit has extended beyond the experiences of black and African women, touching and influencing the entire black community. Many African American males have been nurtured and succored on the strength of the motherwit of black females, as we will note below in the discussion of Frederick Douglass. Before examining this connection between womanist God-talk and motherwit, we must say a word about the emergence of womanist theology in the United States.

Womanist God-Talk in the United States

No development in black religious thought over the past two decades has been more significant than the emergence of womanist God-talk, or womanist theology. Womanist theology developed in the 1980s as an extension of both the black theology and feminist theology movements. Black theology came into being as a formal movement in the late 1960s; its beginning is traced most directly to the publication of James H. Cone's *Black Theology and Black Power* (1969). In this text Cone, echoing the sentiments of many radical black clergy and laypersons, both religious and nonreligious, called into question Western Christianity in general and American Christianity in particular for their witting and unwitting support of the system of racial oppression in the West. His contention was that American churches and theologians had failed because of their inability to address the perennial problem of racism as an inescapable component of American life and history. Cone argued categorically that the race problem was the principal malady in American society. What he and others said about the question of race was directly related to the emergence of feminist theology. Like black liberation theologians, feminist theologians raised major questions about the structure of American Christianity and its allegiance to the oppressive sociocultural structure of Western society. According to feminists, however, the central problem in America was that of sexism and the oppression of women. They insisted that black male theologians were particularly shortsighted in their inability to see the connection between racial oppression and gender inequity. Thus feminists set out to write theology from their vantage point, reflecting their personal and collective experiences as victims of sexual oppression. The range of early feminist theology covers the spectrum from the post-Christian musings of Mary Daly to the critical but more traditional works of Rosemary Ruether.

Womanist theology owes its existence in great measure to black and feminist theologies. Womanist thinkers universally base their God-talk on a statement taken from the words of Alice Walker in her work *In Search of Our Mothers' Gardens: Womanist Prose* (1983); but Walker's Pulitzer Prize–winning novel *The Color Purple* is also frequently used by many womanists. Walker developed the term "womanist" to denote a specific type of thinking, being, and acting drawn from the lived experiences of African American women, thus distinguishing them from white females and both black and white males. Walker gives the following descriptions of the submeanings of the term:

A black feminist or feminist of color. From the black folk expression of mothers to female children, "You acting womanish," i.e., like a woman. Usually referring to outrageous, audacious, courageous or willful behavior. Wanting to know more than is considered "good" for one. Interested in grown-up doings. Acting grown up. . . . A woman who loves other women, sexually and/or nonsexually. Appreciates and prefers women's culture, women's emotional flexibility (values tears as natural counterbalance of laughter) and women's strength. Sometimes loves individual men, sexually and/or nonsexually. . . . Loves music. Loves dance. . . . Loves the Folk. Loves herself. Regardless.[6]

The aspect of this definition that is most often referred to by womanist theologians is the emphasis on black women's experiences and self-love. Taking the cue from Walker, then, womanist God-talk proposes that the historical experiences of black women in America place them in a sad position of triple jeopardy, being oppressed because of their race (a link to black men), their sex (a link to all women), and their socioeconomic class (a bond with poor women around the world). With this recognition as the point of departure, womanist God-talk is religious reflection drawn from the particularity of the social plight of black women. The specific experiences most often referenced by womanist thinkers run the gamut of black life, but principal among them are the fiction, the folk wisdom, the spiritual narratives and autobiographies, and the patterns of parenting and nurturing. More than black male theologians, womanists have creatively and unapologetically probed the depths of the experiences of black women in the New World. Thus the stories and experiences of black women are principal resources for doing womanist theology.

Most womanist theologians are theoretically rooted within the mainstream of the Judeo-Christian tradition despite some of their differences regarding specific points of doctrine. For the purposes of this study, the central fact about womanist thought that needs to be considered is its emphasis on the primacy of black women's experiences as the principal locus and source of its religious reflections. One can turn to James H. Cone and Gayraud S. Wilmore's *Black Theology: A Documentary History: Volume 2 (1980–1992)* for a thorough introduction to the varying perspectives among womanist theologians and a concise discussion of some of the recent scholarship in this area. The common bond between womanist thought and the motherwit traditions that is being accented in this essay is the emphasis on the visions, wisdom, and plight of African American women.

Womanist God-Talk and Motherwit: Historical and Literary Motifs

In the area of religious experience, womanist thought and motherwit wisdom are most intimately connected by their common understanding of religious experience. More specifically, these two traditions focus upon black women's power to name their own experience of the Divine. Delores S. Williams speaks of womanist God-talk in terms of Christian theology ("having that little talk with Jesus . . . who makes a way out of no way"),[7] but for my purposes womanist God-talk is inclusive of Christian and non-Christian experiences with the Divine, given our African heritage and the simultaneous effects of racism, sexism, classism, homophobia, and other oppressions of women of African descent. This has become clear to me from my own "talk" with the Divine through visions and research. The Divine spoke to me while I was a student at Albany State College in Georgia, in 1971, asking, "Do you want to be a teacher and sail on the ships of this world, or a preacher and sail on the portals of heaven?" When I answered, "A preacher," the Divine voice promised, "This shall be because you have patience and you can wait . . . and when I do this it shall be meant for all!" Again, in 1986, while I was a graduate student at Drew

University just prior to my African research in Nigeria, the Divine voice said to me, "I am Olodumare," which was later interpreted for me as "God Almighty" in the Yoruba language.

God's breaking through and speaking to us in our experiences is not new for black women. There are many instances of it in the testimonies of black women in southern religion, whose voices too often are stifled by oppressive forces. *Ase* (Yoruba for the "creative power to make things happen"[8]) remains vital within womanist God-talk and religious experience, which is why so many African American women can relate to the African slave Hagar and the Divine voice that made "a way out of no way" for her and her son Ishmael in the wilderness. Consequently, much of motherwit contains stories revolving around Hagar and Ishmael; African American slave mothers passed this wisdom on to subsequent generations in acts of survival, faith, and determination, creating in America— especially the southern United States—a quasi-African sacred cosmos.[9] In this cosmos, the stories of Hagar's motherwit reveal the Divine as family. This is best exemplified in a popular saying of the black religious tradition: "God, you've been a father and mother to me, sister and a brother"), that transcends the subservience encouraged by the slaveholder's religion and making of religion their own unique protest movement. I call this tradition of motherwit the "wilderness motif," because the Divine deals with oppressed women in the wilderness of our lives and gives us new survival tactics out of old sources.

It took me years of research in African and African American religious understandings of the sacred cosmos to begin to deal with the confluences of gender in sacred and secular texts that address wilderness and exodus motifs. We who are of African descent, before colonization and conversion to religions such as Christianity and Islam, have a sense of the Divine that includes a notion of a Universal Spirit. The Yoruba tradition, for example, includes a belief in such spiritual powers as Olodumare and messenger spirits such as Yemoja (the female deity of the seas and of fertility), Oya (female deity of the cemetery, whirlwind, transformation, and militaristic retribution), Iyanla (the female Great Mother of the sacred cosmos), and Ogun (the powerful male deity of iron and of war). We did not just drop these understandings off in the Atlantic Ocean during the Middle Passage, our trek into the modern diaspora experience of African peoples. Rather, African retentions reemerge in the sacred and secular motifs of African Americans (contrary to the hypotheses of E. Franklin Frazier and others who follow in his scholarly footprints).

Hagar, the Egyptian *shifhah* (a term that identifies her as the hand-maiden or woman servant, *am ah*, of Sarah, not just the concubine of Abraham [Genesis 16:1–5 and 21:1–21]), may be an example of matrifocality in the "matriliny" that stretches from Hagar and Ishmael through the Hagarites and continues through the African descendants in the United States (particularly in the South). One common thread flows throughout this wilderness motif of motherwit and womanist God-talk: the cry of Hagar and Ishmael. They are seen and heard by the Divine, who revives them and shows them how to use old sources to make a "way out of no way." Many slave mothers and grandmothers throughout the South could relate to Hagar's and Ishmael's womanist God-talk and motherwit. Hagar goes on to name the well of living water for her god/goddess (*Beer-lahai-ro'i*, "well of the living one that sees me," in the sense of theophany). Savina J. Teubal challenges us (as does Williams) to deconstruct from a womanist-feminist point of view who prior exegetes have determined the Divine in this instance to be either the male YHWH, Elohim, or the male local god of the mountains *El Shaddai*). However, Teubal further points out that without the *El*, *shaddai* can come from the root of *shadeh* or *shadad*, meaning "from the breasts," and thus raising the possibility that female deities were worshiped.[10] For many slaves of African descent this would be similar to relating to female deities such as Yemoja (mother goddess of the ocean so many slaves crossed over), Oya (mother goddess of transformation and the whirlwinds of life), or Osun (the river fertility deity) in the Yoruba cosmology. Even in the slave environment, under excruciating circumstances, the female knowledge of these deities was passed on and preserved in places such as Louisiana, Florida, South Carolina, Virginia, and even New York.

Similarly, Williams notes the Egyptian god Ra, whose eye was capable of searching out people in the wilderness of oppression and becoming as Hathor to them, was the mother goddess capable of both good and destruction. Many traditional African religions are comprised of female and male deities who are not necessarily exclusive, and certainly these deities possess the simultaneous powers of good and evil. Hathor becomes the surrogate for Ra in much the same way the Egyptian Hagar serves as the surrogate for Sarah, and in much the same way many slave women served as surrogates for white oppressors (male and female). It would have been perfectly plausible, Williams further reminds us, for this divinity not to liberate Hagar immediately (as was the experience of many slave women in the South) but rather give her new ways of "seeing" old sources of oppression. This divinity instructs Hagar to return to her oppressors, for both Abraham and Sarah are her oppressors just as white men and white women and in some cases black men remain the oppressors of so many black women in Africa and throughout the diaspora. This divinity then offers Hagar survival wisdom or motherwit until she can be liberated. While an analysis of Williams's work challenges us with problematic ques-

tions of theodicy and whether the nature of the Divine is arbitrarily oppressive or liberating, Williams accepts the truism, as do many black
women, that "God is . . . or God does as God wills," and we must find
ways of coping within this reality. Such ways may involve "praying for the
welfare of oppressors and oppressed" until our fair share can be gained.[11]
Even today, in the African American community, it is commonplace to
hear references to persons who had no formal educational training but
were nonetheless successful because they had motherwit, the survival
wisdom and skills of our people. These people know how to survive and
thrive despite their desperate socioeconomic and political circumstances.
This is motherwit. This is in the best spirit of womanist God-talk.

The connection between motherwit, or womanist God-talk, and
southern religion is often best demonstrated in narrative form. One example appears in the autobiography of Harriet Jacobs, *Incidents in the Life of a
Slave Girl.* From about the time she was six years old, the mulatto Harriet
Jacobs was owned by cruel masters, Dr. and Mrs. Flint. Until Harriet was
around nineteen, Dr. Flint sought to make her his mistress. She rebuked
his attempts but nevertheless incurred the scorn of his jealous wife, who
was aware of her husband's infatuation. Harriet suffered a severe loss of
self-esteem and entered into an affair with a Mr. Sands (who is believed
to be in fact the attorney and legislator Samuel Treadwell). From this
liaison she had two children, Benny and Ellen.

Throughout this slave narrative the reader is impressed by the deep
affinity between Harriet and Aunt Martha (her grandmother), who gained
her freedom in the South during slavery, maintained her own home, and
lived to see the freedom of her grandchildren and great-grandchildren.
Harriet's grandmother had an abiding faith in the Divine, who would, at
the right time, free the enslaved to go "where the wicked shall cease from
Troublin" (a metaphor for heaven or for freedom "at the North"). Harriet's grandmother believed that no matter how cruel slavery might be (it
caused the death of her own daughter, Aunt Nancy, who experienced six
miscarriages under adverse conditions), God would still make a way out
of no way by somehow enabling her remaining family to be free.[12] For her,
patient trust in the Divine was necessary for survival, and indeed she
outlived most of her family.

Harriet too believed in patience, but she also felt that the Divine
moves in the midst of difficult circumstances if we put faith into action.
She confronted Mr. Sands and demanded freedom for her children, which
he eventually allowed. Harriet herself spent over seven years as a fugitive
slave, running from the law and hiding in her grandmother's storage room
off the roof. There she prayed, watched her children grow, took what
meals she could, listened constantly to the voices of her oppressors, and

never gave up her plan to escape to freedom in the North. Her opportunity came when her friend Peter arranged a voyage for Harriet and her friend Fanny to Philadelphia and eventually to New York and England. Through all of this, Harriet believed that "God so orders circumstances."[13]

Harriet's initial wilderness was not liberation to the North; rather, in spite of her circumstances, in the midst of her persecutors in the South, in her grandmother's shed, where for over seven years she prayed, cried, waited, and prepared for the right time for her exodus. She remained active in naming her own experiences and insisting that God alone knew how she "suffered." During her own womanist God-talk in her wilderness experience, Harriet was constantly strengthened by the motherwit of her grandmother, passed through the cracks in a garret shed where she could barely stand up straight. Then and during her sojourn later in Snaky Swamp, her imposture as a white sailor, and the threat of death if she were caught (especially strong because of the uprisings over the Nat Turner rebellions), Harriet did not sink into total despair. Like Hagar, she received from her tribulations new visions for handling old oppressive forces until she was able to escape. Harriet believed the Divine saw and heard her and would make a way when there seemed to be none.

Just as Harriet's grandmother became a source of motherwit, so does Nanny (Janie's grandmother) in Zora Neale Hurston's book *Their Eyes Were Watching God.* Here again the setting is in the deep South, but now in the early twentieth century. Even though physical slavery has ended, Hurston deals with enslavement to the forces of patriarchy that can be just as deadly for black women. Here we have a concise stating of the facts of life with respect to interstructured oppression:

> Honey de white man is de ruler of everything as fur as Ah been able tuh find out. . . . So de white man throw down de load and tell de nigger man tuh pick it up. He pick it up because he have to, but he don't tote it. He hand it to his women folks. De nigger women is de mule uh de world so fur as Ah can see. Ah been prayin' fuh it tuh be different wid you. Lawd, Lawd, Lawd![14]

As if by the violent slap Nanny gives Janie, the reader is shocked, jolted into the realities of being black and female without the luxury of playing the sexual field with Logan Killicks, Johnny Taylor, Teacake, or any man. Nanny does not want Janie's life controlled by white men *or* black men, as the lives of so many black women have been. Nanny is a prime example of what I have come to call an "unchurched preacher," passing on wisdom to her offspring Janie and, indeed, to the world.

As Nanny holds the crying Janie in her arms, she explains and preaches in a running chain prayer:

> You know honey, us colored folks is branches without roots and that makes things come round in queer ways. You in particular. Ah was born back due in slavery so it wasn't for me to fulfill my dreams of whut a woman ought a be and to do. Dat's one of de hold-backs of slavery. But nothing can't stop you from wishin'. You can't beat nobody down so low till you can rob 'em of they will. Ah didn't want mah daughter used tat way neither. It sho wasn't mah will for things to happen lak they did. Ah even hated de way you was born. But, all de same Ah said thank God, Ah got another chance. Ah wanted to preach a great sermon about colored women sit tin' on high, but they wasn't no pulpit for me. Freedom found me wid a baby daughter in mah arms, so Ah said Ah'd take a broom and a cook-pot and throw up a highway through de wilderness for her. She would expound what Ah felt. But somehow she got lost off a de highway and next thing Ah know Ed here you was in de world. So whilst Ah was tendin' you of nights Ah said Ah'd save de text for you. Ah been wait in' a long time, Janie, but no thin' Ah been through ain't too much if you just take a stand on high ground lak Ah dreamed.[15]

As Nanny continues to rock Janie, she expounds the dreams of many black mothers and grandmothers that their daughters will have the best in the world. She shows the pain they feel (womanist God-talk moan of "Lawd, Lawd, Lawd!") when those dreams are shattered in the reality of a world that cares nothing for black women except to treat us like "mules of the world." Yet despite these realities, Nanny—as many other grandmothers and mothers have done with African American females—continues to express her divine wisdom, hoping that Janie will partake of it at some point and stand on the "high ground."

In rereading Hurston's words I could not help but think of the many womanist preachers who are denied the benefit of an official pulpit simply because they are women. These women are oppressed not only by white patriarchy and matriarchy but by our own African American denominational churches which have practiced egregious oppression all too many times in the South and the North. These churches colonize the minds and spirits of black women, who often make up more than 75 percent of the congregations across all denominations, while denying them adequate clergy representation by their own gender. Yet like Nanny, these women continue to throw up their own pulpits in the wilderness of life and to make a way out of no way.

Finally, motherwit and womanist God-talk came together in the
grandmother Baby Suggs in Toni Morrison's *Beloved*. Because slave life
has "busted her legs, head, eyes, hands, kidneys, womb and tongue," she
becomes the "unchurched preacher" with whom many of us womanist
theologians can identify, both in the South and in the North. Out of the
depths of her own being, she connects with the Divine, not through insti-
tutionalized sacred texts but from creation itself, making a living by opening her "great big heart." Like Hagar, Harriet Jacobs, and Nanny, Baby
Suggs uses in a new, liberating way the natural resources we all possess.
Her wilderness is a simple "clearing" in nature. Here she cuts through
the denominationalism of "AME's . . . Baptists, Holinesses, Sanctifieds,
Church of the Redeemer and Redeemed." She cuts through the divisions
between black men, women, and children. She is "uncalled, unrobed,
unanointed," and yet she lets "her great heart beat in their presence." I
can imagine her heart beating the rhythms of Africa, the degradation of
intertribal warfare, the colonization of the slave diaspora, the despair of
Margaret Garner (who cuts the throat of her child rather than have that
child endure slavery). It is the rhythmic beating that tells the story of
African American wilderness and exodus oppressions (including the
shameful story of our oppression of each other), a beating that refuses to
be silenced!

Out there in the natural surroundings, deeply in touch with the clearing of the land and the "ringing trees" (many African peoples believe that
trees communicate especially to wood-carvers), "Let the children come!"
They run from the trees to her "heart." "Let your mothers hear you
laugh" after the weeping of so many ages. "Let the grown men come"
from the "ringing trees." "Let your wives and your children see you
dance," she commands them, as they shake the ground, the natural source
of life underneath their feet. And then to the women, "Cry . . . for the
living dead. . . . Just cry." This is her sermon, expressing those natural
emotions as a reclamation of life, as Hagar did in her wilderness and well-
spring experience. In conclusion, she pronounces her final benediction,
like so many womanists before her, naming her own experience, bringing
together the sacred and secular, spirit and flesh. It is, I believe, the substance of womanist reflection, God-talk, and motherwit:

> Love your flesh . . . flesh that weeps, laughs, flesh that dances on
> bare feet in grass. Love it. Love it hard. Yonder they do not love
> your flesh. They despise it. . . . And O my people. . . . This is flesh
> I'm talking about here. Flesh that needs to be loved. . . . The dark,
> dark liver—love it, love it, and the beat and beating heart, love that
> too![16]

The Universality of Motherwit
in the African American Experience

The strength and depths of the motherwit tradition in the African American community are furthered by the fact that motherwit is also passed on across gender lines. In *Mother Wit*, Ronnie W. Clayton provides an excellent demonstration of the universal motif in the motherwit tradition. His work focuses on the wit and wisdom in the narratives of former Louisiana slaves.[17] In describing the experiences of these former slaves, Clayton uses a slightly different definition of the term "motherwit" and different spelling from what I have used in this essay. He notes the following example of one African American description of the universal meaning of motherwit:

> I got Mother Wit instead of an education. Lots of colored people in offices and school don't seem to know what Mother Wit is. Well, it's like this: I got a wit to teach me what's wrong. I got a wit to not make me a mischief-maker. I got a wit to keep people's trusts. No one has to tell me not to tell what they say to me in confidence, for I respect what they say, and I never tell. I'm glad I had good raisin'.[18]

While the emphasis here covers a broader scope of experiences than I have discussed specifically as an expression of African American female wisdom, the central idea, namely the idea of an African American folk wisdom tradition, is maintained. In this last segment of the essay, I will talk briefly about motherwit and its more general setting within the African American experience.

One has only to read the writings of Frederick Douglass to understand how women such as his mother and grandmother passed on to him the motherwit spirit discussed thus far in this study. Douglass was born a slave in Tuckahoe, Maryland, around 1817. He wrote with great fondness about both of his grandparents but used special terms of endearment for his grandmother Betsey Baily and his mother, Harriet. He knew nothing of his biological father, and he was cut off from close intimacy with his mother; but what he did know of her remained with him for life. Betsey Baily was a woman of great wisdom and strength. Douglass remembered her reputation as a loving grandmother; she reared the children of her biological offspring, all of whom, like Douglass's mother, were sold to planters from other plantations.[19] Grandmother Betsey was known for her homespun wisdom and wit, which she willingly shared with her children and grandchildren. She was particularly influential upon young Frederick, who gave her, along with his grandfather Isaac, credit for having saved him from some of the harshness of slavery. Douglass would later write that "it was a long time before I knew myself to be a slave"[20] because of the warmth and security that he felt in the home of his grandparents. He felt like a free person, though he was living in a cabin on a plantation.

Grandmother Betsey was, in Douglass's estimation, one of the "greatest people in the world."[21] Her ability to survive led others to assert that she was lucky, but according to Douglass, she also had wit, which she exhibited, along with her wisdom and survival skills, among both slaves and freedpersons. She was particularly skilled in fishing and farming. Douglass states that her ability to make fishing nets and catch fish was legendary. She was able to sell many of her nets to people from neighboring villages, and she spent a great deal of her time fishing, often catching enough to supplement her family's diet. In gardening, she specialized in sweet potatoes. So adept was she at working with potatoes that some people believed if "Grandmamma Betsey but touches them at planting, they will be sure to grow and flourish."[22] Her willingness to help others did not go unnoticed; in return, people gave her a percentage of their profits and yield. Douglass notes, in fact, that his grandmother maintained an autonomous financial base, being free to make and use her money as she pleased. And she always used her excess and resources to care for the numerous children on her plantation, who were often undernourished.

When Douglass later reflected on the hardships of slaveocracy, one of the things that he bemoaned most was the degree to which it separated families and obliterated the creative efforts and contributions of women such as his grandmother. She fought against the system all her life, but in the end even she could not escape its overwhelming grasp. Douglass was flabbergasted at the way his grandmother was treated at the end of her life by her owners.

> She had served my old master faithfully from youth to old age. She had been the source of all his wealth; she had peopled his plantation with slaves; she had become a great-grandmother in his service. She had rocked him in infancy, attended him in childhood, served him through life, and at his death wiped from his icy brow the cold death-sweat, and closed his eyes forever. She was nevertheless left a slave—a slave for life—a slave in the hands of strangers; and in their hands she saw her children, her grandchildren, and her great-grandchildren, divided, like so many sheep, without being gratified with the small privilege of a single word, as to their or her own destiny.[23]

The height of the indignity against Grandmother Betsey came when she was isolated at the end of her life in "a little hut" in the woods. Despite all of her gifts and contributions, she was left without the things that she cherished most, family and friends: "If my poor old grandmother now lives, she lives to suffer in utter loneliness; she lives to remember and mourn over the loss of children, the loss of grandchildren, and the loss of great-grandchildren."[24]

Douglass's statements about his grandmother tell much about the motherwit spirit that I have been examining in this study, about its connection to black life and how it transcended gender, touching every facet of black life on plantations. It is no accident that Douglass had such fond memories of her and of the impact she made on his life.

Douglass's mother, Harriet, also demonstrated the motherwit spirit that he admired so much in his grandmother. Though she was sold out to work on another plantation twelve miles away, she refused to allow this separation to prohibit her from being with her son. At night, after having worked during the day, she walked the twelve miles each way to see Douglass and, in defiance to the obstacles imposed by slaveocracy, provided him with an important source of strength. Douglass recalled that on one occasion, Aunt Katy, a cook, had punished him by starving him all day. His mother appeared later with a "ginger cake," and "she read aunt Katy a lecture which she never forgot." She threatened to complain to Master Lloyd. The young Douglass understood the implications of this act very well and drew considerable strength from his mother's determination and protectiveness: "The friendless and hungry boy, in his extremist need—and when he did not dare to look for succor—found himself in the strong, protecting arms of a mother; a mother who was, at the moment (being endowed with high powers of manner as well as matter) more than a match for all his enemies."[25] Though he was cut off from his mother to some extent, Douglass learned much from observing her persistence and dedication to caring for her family, as he did from his grandmother. This is the essence of motherwit, the will to survive, the determination to "make do while don't prevails."

In the essays in this volume by Alonzo Johnson and William C. Johnson, there are additional areas where the motherwit of black women might be identified. I have referred to women's experiences in African American religious communities. The discussions about the development of folk institutions and practices among African American southerners demonstrate another sphere in which women's wisdom, wit, and experiences have influenced their communities. In their various functions as seekin' mothers, church mothers, spiritual mothers, prayer-bands leaders, and the like, black women have provided spiritual structure, strength, and meaning for their communities for centuries. There is room for even more research in this area. William C. Johnson's reflections on the morality of the

Brer Rabbit tales also capture a critical aspect of the folk life of African Americans. These tales can be read equally as a strong demonstration of the universalization of motherwit in African American life. Whatever one's opinion about the specific origins, morality, and symbolism of the tales, the fact remains that they communicate something about the survival spirit and collective wisdom of the African American community. Though the characters in them are not females, their ability to fight against great odds, accept challenges, and use wit, cunning, wisdom, and experience in combating their enemies demonstrate the essence and depth of the motherwit motif in black African American life.

Notes

The author wishes to acknowledge the substantial contribution made by Alonzo Johnson to the final version of this essay.

1. Delores S. Williams, *Sisters in the Wilderness: The Challenge of Womanist God-Talk* (Maryknoll, N.Y.: Orbis Books, 1993), title page.
2. Ibid., 34.
3. Melville Herskovits, *The Myth of the Negro Past* (Boston: Beacon Press, 1958).
4. See Robert Farris Thompson, *Flash of the Spirit: African and Afro-American Art and Philosophy* (New York: Vintage Books, 1984); Joseph E. Holloway, ed., *Africanisms in American Culture* (Bloomington and Indianapolis: Indiana University Press, 1991); Mechal Sobel, *Trabelin' On: The Slave Journey to an Afro-Baptist Faith* (Westport, Conn.: Greenwood Press, 1979).
5. E. Franklin Frazier, *The Negro Family in the United States* (New York: Dryden Press, 1948), 119.
6. Alice Walker, *In Search of Our Mothers' Gardens: Womanist Prose* (New York: Harcourt Brace Jovanovich, 1983), xi–xii.
7. Williams, *Sisters in the Wilderness*, ix–12.
8. Thompson, *Flash of the Spirit*, 5.
9. Sobel, *Trabelin' On*, 3–57.
10. Savina J. Teubal, *The Lost Tradition of the Matriarchs: Hagar the Egyptian* (San Francisco: HarperCollins, 1992) 26–37; Williams, *Sisters in the Wilderness*, 6.
11. Williams, *Sisters in the Wilderness*, 24–25, 71, 193–203.
12. Harriet Jacobs (pseudonym Linda Brent), *Incidents in the Life of a Slave Girl* (New York: Oxford University Press, 1988; originally published in 1861).
13. Ibid., 303.
14. Zora Neale Hurston, *Their Eyes Were Watching God*; (Chicago: Lippincott, 1978; originally published in 1937), 29–32.
15. Ibid., 31–32.
16. Toni Morrison, *Beloved* (New York: Plume, 1987), 87–88.

17. See Ronnie W. Clayton, *Mother Wit: The Ex-Slave Narratives of the Louisiana Writers' Project* (New York: Peter Lang, 1990).
18. Ibid. See the preface.
19. Frederick Douglass, *My Bondage and My Freedom* (New York: Miller, Orton and Mulligan, 1855).
20. Ibid., 38.
21. Ibid., 35–36.
22. Ibid.
23. Ibid., 180.
24. Ibid.
25. Ibid., 56.

Black Methodist Preachers in the South Carolina Upcountry, 1840–1866

Isaac (Counts) Cook, James Porter, and Henry McNeal Turner

Stephen W. Angell

The best black Methodist ministers in the South Carolina Upcountry during the mid-nineteenth century were powerful preachers who made their mark by both profound piety and effective oratory. That, at least, was the viewpoint of Henry McNeal Turner, an Upcountry native who became a Methodist minister during that time. "The old time preachers read the Bible, committed hundreds of chapters to memory, scores of hymns, fasted, prayed, and we have seen them bring more souls to God in one sermon than three-fourths of our present preachers do in a year," Turner wrote in 1897. "These men preached under the illuminations of the Holy Ghost."[1] The purpose of this essay is to assess Turner's claims against the background of admittedly fragmentary evidence relating to the work of black preachers in the South Carolina Upcountry during the days of slavery. In recent decades, the scholarly literature on mid-nineteenth-century black preachers has grown substantially, but little of it has focused specifically on the Upcountry region of South Carolina.[2]

Many of the black Methodist preachers were individuals who worked at other careers that already marked them as leaders in the black community. Henry Brown of Columbia remembered that his father, Abraham, a preacher who was very successful in obtaining conversions from his listeners, had also been the driver, or head man, at a local plantation.[3] When William Brown, an African Methodist Episcopal (AME) minister from Baltimore, assumed leadership of the largest Columbia black Methodist congregation in 1866, he was pleased to find that there were thirteen local preachers in his congregation and more persons who were licensed to exhort (Methodist exhorters often delivered short sermons, in a similar fashion to those who were licensed to preach). They were a "noble set of Christian brethren," Brown exclaimed. One of the local preachers was Mr. Wilder, a head carpenter. William Simons and Mr. Edwards also combined jobs as skilled artisans with their ministerial callings.[4] These Columbia Methodists had been members of the Friendly Union Society, probably a mutual aid and self-improvement association, founded in 1853. Turner praised Columbia's black Methodist ministers as "men of large minds and comprehensive intellects."[5]

These men were the last generation of black preachers in South Carolina to have their spiritual formation, including education and licensure, largely supervised by white ministers. Although the Methodist Episcopal Church had ordained some black Americans as local deacons prior to 1820, it is evident that white Methodists, in the North and South, were ordaining very few, if any, black Methodists to the ministry during the years 1840 to 1861 unless these ministerial aspirants were willing to emigrate to Liberia.[6] Some black Methodist men, however, were licensed as preachers and exhorters or appointed as class leaders in the churches. Although black congregations and most black-attended worship services were strictly supervised by whites, black Methodists were, for the most part, not bereft of some form of black spiritual leadership. The independent black churches, such as the AME Church, did not reestablish their presence in South Carolina until 1863. (The Charleston AME Church, founded in 1817, had been disbanded five years later after the white government accused it of complicity in the Denmark Vesey conspiracy.) The independent black Methodists did not establish a presence in the South Carolina Upcountry until 1865.[7]

Many mid-century black preachers had a slender education at best. It was considered desirable—by their black listeners, at least—for these preachers to be able to read the Bible and the hymnbook. Tony Murphy of Columbia was one preacher who had attained at least this level of literacy; probably Sigh Williams also could read this much.[8] But if the laws of the slave regime, which prohibited teaching literary skills to black Americans under the pretext of averting slave revolts, prevented that attainment by their ministers, they were not necessarily a hindrance. Some black preachers were illiterate but had managed to memorize large portions of the Bible and thus consequently could hold their audiences spellbound by their colorful, insightful, and often quite detailed expositions of Scripture. AME preacher Abram Weston recalled visiting Kitt Stand, a small hamlet outside of Newberry, in 1866 or 1867. The regular preacher was an old man, then esteemed as "a great biblical preacher." Weston, however, had to preach the sermon, and nowhere could he find a Bible or hymnbook to consult. Still, Weston was able to line out the hymns and recite his biblical text from memory, presumably the method that the regular preacher also used to conduct worship services.[9] Both the absence of books and the reliance on memory that Weston relates in this story were typical occurrences for mid-nineteenth-century black preachers in South Carolina. A. M. French, a missionary at Port Royal in the Sea Islands, wrote about the great benefit that the slaves received from black preachers, most of them fellow slaves. These preachers possessed "deep spiritual experience, sound sense, and capacity to state Scripture facts, narratives, and doctrines, far better than most, who feed upon commentaries. True, most of them could not read, still, some of them line hymns from memory with great accuracy, and fervor, and repeat Scripture most appropriately, and correctly."[10]

In 1866 Henry McNeal Turner met a forty-year-old black preacher in Georgia who had an extraordinary command of the Bible, despite being illiterate. "I found he almost knew the Bible from memory," wrote Turner. "The man is equal to Cruden's Concordance. He could refer to every chapter and verse in the Bible on any subject whatever, and read chapters and entire books through by memory."[11] Another such minister was Andrew Brown, a Methodist in Georgia. Brown, whose preaching career extended from about 1850 until his death in 1887, was illiterate but also known for his mastery of the Bible. Like his famous contemporary, Baptist preacher John Jasper of Virginia, Brown was known for his exposition of Joshua's command for the sun to stand still. Using a term that the railroads were currently bringing into prominence, Brown stated in one sermon that "God blowed 'down brakes' on the sun"; he was known thereafter as "Down Brakes" Brown.[12] Even those preachers who were able to read still memorized the Bible. Tony Murphy could read the Bible, but he still knew it "almost by memory." Murphy, whose skin was very black, "was the greatest preacher I ever listened to or ever expect to," wrote Turner. "Men of the highest rank and greatest learning hung upon his lips, as God's word was poured forth from his massive mouth, like children." Sanky Taylor could compose an hour-long sermon on any subject "simply by quoting Scripture."[13]

This combination of excellent speaking abilities with extensive use of memory may have partially replicated griot traditions of storytelling from many West African cultures. "As early Black preachers took their texts from their bare hands, open to resemble a Bible held," Henry H. Mitchell has written, "what seemed prodigious biblical memory was only a quick exchange of similar African and Biblical oral testimony."[14] While black preachers shared a biblical basis for their ministry with white preachers, the former derived the style for their ministry largely from Africa, not Europe.

As black folklore from the period will attest, not all uneducated preachers were highly respected by their black congregations. Some of the uneducated preachers were labeled by their listeners as "jackleg" preachers. They were apparently not as spiritually or intellectually gifted as their ministerial colleagues of the first rank, but they still fulfilled important pastoral and liturgical functions. Some were ridiculed because they were thought to be stupid. Thus John Collins of Winnsboro derided the jackleg preacher who could not figure out that a person born on leap day would have only one-fourth the number of birthdays that others had.[15] Also labeled as a jackleg preacher was a man who was instructed by his white boss to lead other slaves in the singing of tunes while working in the cotton fields. Some of the songs he started were spirituals, such as "Got to Fight the Devil When You Come Up out of the Water." Some preachers forfeited the respect of many lay people when they engaged in sexual promiscuity or habitual drunkenness.[16] Those who presided over the weddings of slaves were sometimes characterized as jackleg preachers, perhaps because the ceremonies that they presided over were lacking in dignity; the words used to consummate the marriage were too few, and such embarrassing rituals as jumping over the broomstick were incorporated into the ceremony, perhaps at the insistence of white onlookers. Some of these preachers may have undertaken their ministerial responsibilities out of a sense of duty to their community, which needed someone to assume the mantle of spiritual leadership, rather than out of a sense of inner direction; hence their hastiness in performing the liturgy may have been related to the reluctance with which they undertook their vocation.[17] Howard Thurman observed that sometimes jackleg preachers "were the butt of insensitive jokes, and on the whole, they and their families were not treated with the respect they deserved. However, they endured and kept alive the flickering flame of the spirit when the harsh winds blew and the oil was low in the vessel."[18]

In regard to aspiring illiterate ministers, black Americans had no hesitation in distinguishing between those who were fit for their responsibilities and those who were not. For example, even the venerable AME Bishop Daniel A. Payne, a South Carolina native and perhaps the strongest advocate of an educated ministry within black Methodism, made certain that wise, experienced preachers deficient in literacy skills were retained in the ministerial ranks when they switched from the ME Church, South, to the AME Church after emancipation. In contrast, Payne did dismiss young, incompetent preachers from the ministerial ranks.[19]

Outside of Columbia, in the rural areas of the states and the small towns, antebellum black preachers seem often to have preached outside church buildings. Benjamin Russell of Chester recalled that his favorite preacher, Robert Russell, "was allowed sometimes to use the white folks' school, which wasn't much in those days, just a little log house to hold forth in winter." In the summer, Russell preached in a brush arbor topped by pine boughs, as indeed did many other black preachers.[20] Caleb Craig of Winnsboro remembered that he took part in religious services in the slave quarters on Sunday. "Uncle Dick, an old man, was de preacher."[21] Often black preachers would preside at slave weddings and funerals.

The summer camp meetings, largely held outdoors, showcased black preaching with particular effectiveness. "The Up-Country was pre-eminently the region of the camp meeting," wrote Rosser H. Taylor, commenting about both white and black South Carolinians. "The people . . . found opportunity in the camp meeting to give expression to their religious emotions without fear of criticism."[22] Dickson Bruce has suggested that white preachers and black preachers held services on different parts of the campgrounds for audiences of their own races,[23] but I have found little evidence of strict racial separation during these celebrated events. One of the Upcountry's most famous black scions, Henry McNeal Turner, recalled fondly the powerful impact made by white Methodist preachers during summer camp meetings in 1848 and 1851. By way of contrast, a white listener was profoundly moved during a camp meeting by the preaching of Isaac Cook, one of South Carolina's leading antebellum black preachers.[24]

It is clear that the antebellum black preachers, like their successors after the jubilee, were expert at stimulating an audience reaction, or a "shout," but whites who overheard often were annoyed by the shouting and tried to stop it. Louisa Gause of Marion recalled that "when de colored people would get converted in dem days, dey never allowed to praise de Lord wid dey mouth. Had to pray in dey sleeve in dem days."[25] In 1856 Tony Murphy was preaching at a midnight service in Columbia (the occasion was a "sitting up," or wake) when he raised so loud a shout among his congregation that everyone was arrested. As they were taken to the police station, however, they continued shouting and were apparently released in a very short time. An eyewitness, Turner, recalled many years later that "they shouted John Bedell and his police out of their office."[26] Shouting was seen as more acceptable during the summer camp meetings in the outdoors. Isiah Jefferies of Wilkinsville remembered that his mother shouted and sang for three days at one such camp meeting. When his mother and other black Christians shouted very loudly during their baptismal service, slave patrolers came to silence them. However, Jefferies's master and mistress sent the patrolers away and allowed the blacks to "shout and rejoice to the fullest."[27] Jefferies's and Turner's texts do not make the explicit connections, found in some other sources, between black Americans' shouting and engagement in African-inspired holy dances, such as the slow, shuffling movements of the ring shout.[28] Yet the shouting to which they testified bespeaks of a successful effort, over the opposition of some whites, to impart to the mixed-race milieu of summer camp meetings the African-derived custom of making full, unrestricted use of human voices and bodies for praising and worshiping divinity.

Despite the high stakes involved during slavery days, some brave black South Carolinians did not fear conflict with whites over their conduct of religion, confident that evangelical Protestantism was enough of a common bond for members of both races that threatened violence could be averted. For example, Henry McNeal Turner recalled that Sigh Williams, an old-time black South Carolinian minister whose evangelistic skills he especially respected, "sent every member of a white mob that came to break up his meeting home happily converted, except two, who mounted their horses and galloped away."[29] One might wish for more details on Williams and this incident, but unfortunately nothing further is known.

The fear of premature death was never far distant from the mid-nineteenth-century black preacher in South Carolina. The repression sometimes experienced by black preachers could result in terrible consequences. In 1825 William, a black Georgian, often preached to his fellow slaves on his plantation. His master, Mr. Cokergee, who opposed William's preaching, threatened to whip him with five hundred lashes if he did not cease his ministry. William fled across the state line and got as far as Greenville, South Carolina. A white man, Peter Garrison, discovered him in his barn and shot at him with a rifle. William, in turn, struck and killed his assailant in self-defense. For his actions, William was subjected to the horrible punishment of being burned alive.[30] Most premature deaths of preachers, however, were attributable not to the repression of the slave system but to overwork or to any one of the serious diseases that periodically decimated many nineteenth-century American communities. In an 1866 letter from South Carolina, for example, R. H. Cain chronicled the tragic deaths of two leading black Methodist preachers from the Lowcountry. William Newton died of smallpox at Cooper River, and Isaac Gilyard, a notable camp meeting evangelist, of the "country fever" (possibly malaria or yellow fever), "which is very severe in the summer, and sweeps off a great many persons." (Upcountry preachers were less likely to become sick from the latter disease.) While South Carolinians felt grief at the loss of these ministers, they were consoled to some degree by the hope of life together in the hereafter. "Both of these warriors now sleep in Jesus, till the trumpet of Gabriel wakes them, when they shall come forth and say, 'Here, Lord, am I.' "[31]

The preaching skills of black ministers were often so renowned that white ministers sometimes served a sort of apprenticeship with black preachers to learn how to preach. An early example of a black minister who fulfilled this kind of mentoring role was Uncle Toliver, a black Baptist preacher in Salem, Clarke County, Georgia. In 1820 Toliver was assigned a young white Methodist minister with no prior preaching experience, William J. Parks, as his yokefellow in ministry. This team held two appointments each month. Both Toliver and William preached each time, "alternating as to who should lead, the other always closing the services." Toliver's later career is unrecorded, but his pupil went on to an illustrious ministerial career in the Methodist Church.[32]

Isaac (Counts) Cook

Fairly typical of South Carolina's antebellum black preachers was Isaac Cook (also known as Isaac Counts), a black Methodist preacher who lived in Newberry, South Carolina. We know that Cook was "in his prime" about 1840 and that he was elderly but still vigorous in 1880.[33] This description points to a birthdate for Cook between 1800 and 1810; he died after 1882. Little is known about Cook's education, but it does not appear to have been extensive. Before the war, he appears to have been a licensed preacher who spoke mainly at camp meetings and the funerals of slaves, usually (perhaps always) within a fifty-mile radius of Newberry County. After the war he became an itinerant minister and ordained elder for the AME Church, serving in the Columbia, South Carolina, Conference.

Cook was an extremely eloquent and persuasive speaker. A white listener, "Luther," noted that Cook spoke in a "negro dialect" but affirmed that his dialect did not detract from the power of his preaching.[34] In the South Carolina Upcountry, Cook had an excellent reputation as a preacher. Henry McNeal Turner recalled that the first sermon that he ever heard (in 1840 at the age of six) was one delivered by Cook in Newberry. What he remembered was the tremendous respect with which Cook was beheld. He "was looked upon by all as a great man."[35]

Turner's youthful memories did not include Cook's subject matter, but Luther did record a synopsis for one of Cook's sermons. This one was delivered at an antebellum camp meeting at Concord in Edgefield County. Cook chose as his text Jonah 1:6. (When the prophet, evading God's command to preach repentance to Ninevah, fell asleep on a ship besieged by rough seas, the captain shook him awake, demanding, "What meanest thou, O sleeper?") According to his white listener, the black preacher's sincere, forceful sermon penetrated to the deep concerns of salvation and eternal life that lay at the heart of southern Protestant evangelical faith: "His description of a sinner in the ark of carnal security, afloat on the storm-tossed ocean of life, in danger of going to the bottom, and yet asleep and unconscious of peril, was to my boyish mind indescribably awful. I left the place where that sermon was preached under an irresistible conviction that I had listened to a man of God, and that the best thing I could do for myself was to take warning, and seek for refuge in Christ as I had been so faithfully exhorted to do."[36]

The intensely narrative, experiential rhetorical style that Cook employed has long been central to the construction of African American sermons. According to James H. Evans, a black preacher has been expected to probe beneath the simple words of the text to "embody the voice of God, enflesh the Word of the Lord, provide from her or his own depth of being the personal motivations and innermost thoughts of the biblical characters that the biblical writers providentially left unexpressed."[37] Moreover, by drawing a direct comparison from a soul-endangering predicament faced by a biblical character to the perils of hell confronted by sinners in his audience, Cook placed himself firmly in the mainstream of the black folk tradition of preaching.[38] Cook's sermon had been sheer artistry. Like other black preachers of his time, he had fashioned a sermon that was not only "logically irrefutable" but also "artistically and existentially irresistible."[39] Luther needed no such elaborate explanations of what he had heard, however. He simply affirmed that Cook's ministry had been derived from a divine source: "The Spirit of God was upon him."

Luther claimed that Cook's preaching had been instrumental in the conversion of one of Luther's father's slaves named Governor. On one of Cook's visits to Edgefield County, he had preached the funeral sermon of a family servant. Governor "was profoundly impressed" by Cook's message. But Luther's brothers mischievously "crossed him in his good intentions." Passing quickly over the harassment that the pious black man suffered at the hands of young white boys, Luther proceeded to describe the paternalist remedy. The patriarch, not a Christian convert himself, put an end to his sons' harassment of Governor. "If Governor wanted to change his life and live right, they must not hinder him. If the Gospel seeds which had been planted in the heart of his slave had taken root, this work must go on without hindrance by a set of foolish boys."[40]

One cannot escape the impression that, after the Civil War, the aged Cook's evangelistic powers slipped somewhat, although Turner politely maintained in 1880 that "as a preacher, Cook is in his prime yet." One of his younger listeners, Mary Veals, a Newberry resident born in 1865, recalled that Cook "was a good preacher," though obviously not her favorite. Cook was "a very good man," wrote AME Bishop Wayman. Cook did outlive many of his antebellum ministerial colleagues, such as Alfred Devault, who had died at sea on his way to Liberia.[41] But given the fact that the most important part of Cook's preaching career seems to have transpired during the days of slavery, let us, on the basis of the meager available evidence, try to get a sense of the whole. If, in the words of Robert L. Hall, "slave preachers carved out careers by walking the tight-rope between the master's desire for control and the slaves' desire for autonomy,"[42] Cook appears to have been an expert at this process. "Even the horrors of slavery and the rod of oppression did not deter [Cook] from doing [his] Master's work," wrote Turner.[43] James Weldon Johnson's assessment of the black preacher of this era seems applicable to Cook. "The old-time Negro preacher of parts was above all an orator, and in good measure an actor. . . . He preached a personal and anthropomorphic God, a sure-enough heaven and a red-hot hell. His imagination was bold and unfettered. He had the power to sweep his listeners before him."[44]

Cook was no politician, no revolutionary, but he changed lives and elevated the aspirations of his listeners. Through all the tumultuous political events from 1840 to 1880, he maintained his broad acceptability by concentrating his platform remarks on what all southern Protestants, black and white, conceded to be the essence of Christ's gospel. Cook's career was seen as remarkable by Luther and Turner, and it still seems so, especially given the rigid confines of black Americans' lives in antebellum South Carolina.

James Porter

A few southern black ministers were well educated themselves and worked hard to educate other black Americans. One such individual was James Porter, educator, musician, lay minister, tailor, and a Reconstruction-era legislator. Porter was a native South Carolinian, born in Charleston about 1830.[45] How Porter obtained his substantial education we do not know. His connections to the Upcountry were indirect, but because of the great significance of his unusual contributions to the black church and community, little known today, he merits mention here.

At the age of twenty-six, Porter moved from Charleston to Savannah. At that time he was an Episcopalian, and he was largely responsible for the founding of St. Stephens, a black Episcopal Church in Savannah. He was elected chairman of the Board of the Vestry and warden, served as a lay reader, and directed the choir.

Porter opened a school for slaves and free blacks, who were forbidden to receive an education by Georgia's laws. Most of his students were slaves. The knowledgeable, highly cultured Porter taught reading, writing, arithmetic, and music. He was qualified to teach the playing of the piano, organ, guitar, and violin. Soon after the school's opening, Savannah's whites were winking at the law, finding it very fashionable to send their house servants to Porter to receive his instruction. The Upcountry's Henry McNeal Turner heard of Porter's fame and took lessons from him in 1857, and other black Americans from surrounding regions did the same. According to Turner, large numbers of literate black men in the southeastern states had been taught to read by Porter. Many of his students became legislators or ministers during Reconstruction.[46] At the same time, Porter ran a tailor's shop. During his years in Savannah, he became the wealthiest black man in the city. By 1870 he had an estate amounting to seven thousand dollars.

After the Civil War, Porter served in 1866 as vice president of the Equal Rights and Educational Association, an early political organization that mobilized support for the rights of the freed people. His education made him a natural choice to serve in the Georgia House of Representatives, to which he was elected in 1868. He was an active legislator who worked diligently for reform and civil rights, introducing bills on such subjects as reforming the criminal justice system and providing for nondiscriminatory seating on railroads and streetcars.[47] He unsuccessfully sought the job of minister to Liberia in 1872. Still active on the educational front, Professor Porter (as he was titled by Bishop Alexander Wayman) wrote an English grammar book, served as a principal for black high schools in Georgia and Mississippi and as one of the founding trustees for Morris Brown College, and founded a short-lived theological seminary in Bermuda.[48]

For a time, Porter worked ecumenically with all of the black denominations, serving, for example, as the chief choir director for such mass meetings within Savannah's black community as the 1874 memorial service for Charles Sumner.[49] He assiduously worked toward becoming an ordained Episcopal priest, but he was prevented from attaining that goal by racial prejudice in the Episcopal Church. So he joined the AME Church and by 1873 had been ordained an elder in it. During the last two decades of his life, he pastored churches in Georgia, Mississippi, Arkansas, Pennsylvania, Bermuda, and Ontario. Porter died in New York City on September 24, 1895. In his eulogy, his friend Turner recalled that Porter was "exceedingly practical, widely read, deeply pious, and extremely trustworthy (especially on money matters and even by his bitterest enemies)."[50]

Unlike Cook, Murphy, and Brown, Porter did not win fame on the basis of his preaching power. His ordained ministry came relatively late in life, long after he made his mark within the black community. Unlike the other three men, Porter was extensively educated. He was an outstanding example of an educated minister and successfully combined his ecclesiastical leadership with a wide variety of secular pursuits. His diligent nurturance of black religious leadership through his teaching won him a special place of honor in the black church.

Henry McNeal Turner

Henry McNeal Turner was the youngest and the most famous of the black South Carolina Methodist ministers that we are considering here. He became personally acquainted with Cook, Murphy, and Porter at some time during his youth and young manhood, and it would not be inaccurate to state that each in some sense became a role model for him. He combined the orientation of a Cook and a Murphy toward an oratorically powerful ministry, on the one hand, with the orientation of a Porter toward an educationally committed ministry on the other. It was not an easy synthesis for him but rather one that he would struggle to achieve throughout his life.

Born free in 1834 in the rural environs of Newberry, the light-skinned Turner (his father's mother, Julia Turner, was a white plantation owner) experienced a boyhood that combined elements of both oppression and privilege. His mother, Sarah Greer Turner, came from what was "considered the wealthiest of the colored families of the South at that time."[51] Still, she was not allowed to educate her son to read or write, as her neighbors threatened her with legal action unless she fired the tutor she had engaged to instruct him. Turner consequently appears to have made slow educational progress until 1848, when he moved with his mother to Abbeville after his father's death and his mother's remarriage to Jabez Story.[52]

Turner thrived in Abbeville, a larger town than Newberry and one that epitomized many of the contradictions that beset mid-nineteenth-century South Carolina. It was the birthplace of John C. Calhoun, the U.S. senator famous for his ingenious theories (in Turner's words) "to perpetuate a vicious aristocracy at the expense of others of the same blood, and none the better by race."[53] Twelve years after Turner moved there, Abbeville hosted one of the first secessionist conventions, and in 1865 it was the site of Jefferson Davis's last cabinet meeting. Yet it was also the place where Turner received extensive instruction in such subjects as astronomy, geography, history, law, and theology from several young white attorneys. Not coincidentally, this town was a stronghold for those who opposed the state's laws forbidding the teaching of reading and writing to blacks. A young barrister named Robert Fair, almost certainly one of Turner's teachers, blasted laws prohibiting the literacy of black people as "a slur upon the Christian age in which we live" in an 1851 speech to an approving Abbeville Bible Society. Whites' fear of slave revolts, said Fair, was a patently unacceptable reason for evading God's commands that all people read the Bible for their salvation: "Better suffer the utter destruction of the body, than that the soul should dwell in eternal burnings."[54]

It did not hurt young Henry Turner's prospects to be seen as part of a small, free, mulatto elite with strong ties to Abbeville's white, as well as black, community.[55] One of his black contemporaries, Sylvia Cannon, recalled, "Dey white folks didn't never help none of we black people to read en write no time. Dey learn de yellow chillun, but if they catch we black children with a book, dey nearly bout kill us."[56] And while the skin-color favoritism that Cannon described apparently failed to have helped Turner in the rural environs of Newberry, he does appear to have received some benefit from it in Abbeville. As an adult, Turner never had any doubt about his racial identity; he never sought to be white, nor did he attempt to construct a separate caste for mulattos, as some of his contemporaries apparently did.[57] When "the blacks were arrayed against the browns or mulattos" in an 1866 South Carolina election, Turner deplored the intraracial conflicts. "We want representative men, without relation to color, as long as they carry the brand of negro oppression," he wrote. "We want power; it only comes through organization, and organization comes through unity."[58]

At the same time that Fair and other white lawyers were educating him, Turner came under the influence of black evangelists such as Isaac Cook and Tony Murphy and white evangelists such as C. A. Crowell and Samuel Leard—not to mention his mother, Sarah Story, who had undergone her own emotional conversion in 1844. Turner later recalled that he had been a "wild" youth, given to such sins as whiskey drinking, and that he had been denied full membership in the Methodist Church on at least one occasion. Turner also fondly recalled black fiddle players who had entertained him and the "pigeon-wing" dancing in which he had indulged during his youth.[59] Yet God's grace penetrated to his heart, apparently during the camp meetings that were the highlight of many an Upcountry South Carolinian's liturgical year. Fifty years later, Turner would specify July 16, 1849 as the date of his conversion by Methodist preacher Churchman Crowell,[60] but it seems more likely that his powerful Christian commitment was due to a series of profound spiritual experiences over a period of several years. Turner's conversion seems to have followed many of the same steps, including withdrawal, mourning, and religious epiphany, outlined by Alonzo Johnson in his analysis of "seekin' the Lord." It appears that an 1851 sermon by Methodist Samuel Leard, as well as the 1849 revival conducted by Crowell, resulted in religious epiphanies for Turner. To Leard, Turner wrote, "You . . . so stunned me by your powerful preaching that I fell upon the ground, rolled in the dirt, foamed at the mouth and agonized under conviction until Christ relieved me by his atoning blood."[61]

Turner's conversion was accompanied by a vocational calling to preach the gospel, and so he was licensed as an exhorter in 1851. He then led prayer meetings among Abbeville slaves. Two years later, he received a license to preach, something often denied by white Methodists even to clearly qualified black applicants. Sarah Story, a Baptist, had shouted for happiness all night when her son had been converted and then was delighted when he became a Methodist minister. According to Alonzo Johnson's classificatory scheme, Story might be called Turner's "seekin' mother" as well as his biological mother.

Furthermore, Turner was permitted to carry his very successful ministry outside of his home state of South Carolina to black and white congregations in Georgia, Alabama, Mississippi, and Louisiana. A major reason for Turner's evangelistic success throughout much of the South was his unusual synthesis of the strengths of Porter, Cook, and Murphy. Like Porter's, his reading was not restricted simply to the Bible and the hymnbook. Instead, his religious worldview was founded on a voracious, wide-ranging reading of classics such as Milton's *Paradise Lost*, the work of popular Christian theologians such as Thomas Dick, and historical and scientific books. He memorized much of what he read and understood it thoroughly enough to use it in extemporaneous oratory. But he seldom allowed his erudition to detract from his oratory. From Murphy and Cook he had learned how an earnest, biblically-based message eloquently delivered could move listeners and change lives. Thus his ministry in the 1850s appears to have successfully combined both learning and powerful oratory. His sermonic mastery astonished his listeners and moved them to bestow a number of glowing sobriquets upon him. Turner was declared to be a "Negro Spurgeon," after Charles H. Spurgeon, the equally young and tremendously acclaimed English Baptist evangelist of the time. Some of his white listeners declared him to be "a white man galvanized." Turner undoubtedly took pleasure in the broad acclaim that he won; in 1899 he had nostalgic feelings for "the friendly relations that once existed between whites and blacks [in the antebellum South] and that trust that was reposed in the negro."[62]

Like all antebellum black preachers, however, Turner could allude only with the utmost care to topics relating to slavery and freedom. In 1866 he vividly remembered the effects of this terrible self-censorship. He could not have preached the Golden Rule during his preaching tours of the 1850s. "God's word had to be frittered, smeared, and smattered to please the politics of slavery."[63] Of course, the well-informed Turner did take careful note of all of that decade's momentous events, in many of which South Carolinians played a prominent part. He remembered a white minister's prayer in 1851 that all abolitionists should be submerged in the sea of God's wrath.[64] Turner noted the profoundly destabilizing effect wrought on South Carolina by Senator Stephen Douglas's "squatter sovereignty" proposals, which made it conceivable for slavery to be introduced into Kansas.[65] When in 1856 an antislavery Massachusetts senator, Charles Sumner, was beaten and almost killed on the floor of the U.S. Senate by a South Carolina colleague, Preston Brooks, it created a sensation in Brooks's home state. Turner undoubtedly received this news grimly, for later, recalling the event, he referred to South Carolina as "the pestiferous State of my nativity."[66] By 1858, following the infamous Dred Scott decision, there were legislative proposals in virtually every southern state, including South Carolina, to reenslave free blacks like Turner and his wife, Eliza Peacher Turner, whom he had married two years earlier. It was then clear to Turner that the United States was headed for disunion.

> . . . the northern lights, which frescoed the heavens, were [so] terrific in their appearance that the skies would at times seem to be turning with blood, and the hearts of men in every direction failing, from the dreadful foreboding anticipations. . . . The free people of color in every direction were hunted and pursued as rabbits, and particularly in the slave States denounced as an offensive nuisance, while church conventions and conferences broke up in wild confusion, political assemblies . . . ended in partisan strife. The atmosphere of human society seemed to be charged with sectional divisibility, and all avowed obligations which bound man to man appeared to be severed.[67]

Under night skies adorned with the aurora borealis in 1858, Henry and Eliza Turner moved to St. Louis and eventually to Baltimore. In St. Louis the Turners were able to affiliate with an independent black denomination, the AME Church. The risks of remaining in the South were simply too great for them to take.

The next seven years were almost as momentous and change-filled for Turner as they were for the nation. He rapidly advanced within his new denomination, becoming an ordained elder and holding one of its most important pastorates, that of Israel AME Church in Washington, D.C. In 1863 he resigned his pastorate to become one of the first black chaplains in the Union Army.[68] Turner's unusual, varied training and experiential learning in the South and the North helped to shape him into one of the most original, versatile, self-confident, and unorthodox intellectuals in nineteenth-century black America. He returned to the South in December 1865 as an organizer for the AME Church and settled in Macon, Georgia. Like Cook's and Porter's, Turner's postemancipation ministry took place largely within the confines of the South.[69]

Turner was, on the whole, an eloquent defender of African-derived styles of worship and preaching within postwar black Methodist churches. In the late 1860s he seemed mildly critical of shouting, thus placing himself at some distance from the emotional religion of his youth. Emotional conversions, accompanied by physical movements, showed that black churches had been "cursed" with a "moral miasma," he stated in 1865 from North Carolina, where he was stationed as an army chaplain. Most black Christians thought it necessary for a convert to "get a little animated," even if he or she should "kick a few shins . . . [or] knock some innocent person on the nose and set it bleeding; . . . whereas, if the individual had claimed justification under more quiet circumstances, its legitimacy would be doubted." One year later, Turner, then in Georgia, was disinclined to view shouting in church as a moral problem. He still admitted that he was "not much for shouting," but he highly praised a ministerial coworker whose effective preaching aroused shouting and produced conversions.[70]

Soon he returned to a reaffirmation of the emotional religion of his boyhood. In 1875, more than twenty years after his own conversion, he had a very physical religious experience during a visit to his native state. At a revival outside Columbia, he "neighed, and brayed, and bleated, and squealed, and roared, and jumped, and kicked" when the evangelist Benjamin Porter "raised up a shout." A few weeks after this experience, Turner stated that black preachers who wanted to get up a shout possessed a "laudable ambition" because the shout "answers as an inventive to the ignorant and frequently edified those of higher culture." In his *Genius and Theory of Methodist Polity* (1889), he reflected that ministers ought to "preach till men fear, tremble and their knees smite each other and their hearts sink within them; preach till the people weep, cry out, lament their sins, and turn to God." Those who opposed shouting "must be crazy," he stated; he wondered what religion is ever "destitute of emotion."[71] Many of Turner's ministerial contemporaries did not share his later affirmations of shouting. For example, his senior bishop, Daniel Payne, deplored shouting in the black churches. At an 1878 "bush meeting," Payne encountered black worshipers performing a ring shout, and he did not like what he saw. Payne informed them that shouting was "a heathenish way to worship and disgraceful to themselves, the race, and the Christian name."[72]

Occasionally Turner too criticized some Africanisms such as the singing of black spirituals. In the introduction to a hymnbook he compiled for
the AME Church, he criticized the "widespread custom of singing on
revival occasions, especially, what is commonly called SPIRITUAL SONGS,
most of which are devoid of sense and reason; and some are absolutely
false and vulgar." Reviewing a song book published in 1897, Turner
praised it for *excluding* black spirituals in favor of the familiar revival hymns
(or "old Zion songs") that Turner loved.[73] On the impropriety of singing
spirituals, Payne and Turner were in agreement. Payne rejected such
songs, referring to them scornfully as "corn-field ditties."[74]

Aside from his principal residence, which after 1865 was always in
Georgia,[75] Turner felt that he had two homes: Africa and South Carolina.
His love of Africa led him to make four missionary trips there in the 1890s.
Turner's statement that "God is a Negro" both provoked and inspired
his contemporaries while anticipating a major theme of twentieth-century
black theology. Turner's own black theology led him to caution that black
churches should not use a liturgy that degraded blackness:

> We need hymns . . . that will harmonize the purity of black with the
> purity of our religion. Every Sabbath we are singing in all of our
> churches to be washed whiter than snow. . . . Such hymns are de-
> grading if not infernal in their effects upon the Negro race.[76]

Turner's affinity for Africa dated from his earliest childhood. He remembered his grandmother telling him that his grandfather, David Greer,
had been an African prince stolen from the west coast of Africa and sold
as a slave in South Carolina. Not only was he proud of his African heritage,
but, more controversially, he also cherished high hopes for a redeemed
Africa—civilized and Christianized—as a future home for black Americans. There was controversy on this matter even within his own South
Carolina family. His aunt Hannah Greer and his father-in-law, Joseph
Peacher, emigrated to Liberia and lived the rest of their lives there; on the
other hand, Story and Turner's first wife, Eliza Peacher Turner, showed no
interest in emigration and, indeed, were even opposed to Henry Turner's
visiting Africa. (He never did travel to Africa while Story and Eliza Turner
were alive.) While Turner never made Africa his main residence, his enthusiasm for his ancestral continent never waned. His pronouncements on
the subject were definitely religious in tone and content; he stressed that
the return of black Americans to Africa was not only divinely blessed but
also providentially ordained.[77]

None of his enthusiasm for Africa obviated the fact that Turner was
South Carolinian, with important ties to both blacks and white in that

state; indeed, he never denied and often celebrated this part of his heritage. His friend Benjamin Tanner stated that the fact that "Henry McNeale [*sic*] Turner is a South Carolinian . . . readily accounts for all the nervousness, three-fourths of the fire, one-half the eccentricity, and one-quarter the fatuity, found in him."[78] The experience he gained during his antebellum ministry in South Carolina helped to lay a solid foundation for his postwar ministerial, educational, and political career. He developed a network of friends and acquaintances, including Porter, that would be indispensable to him for the rest of his life. When the mature Turner needed a spiritual recharge, he often returned to his boyhood haunts in South Carolina. In July 1899, on the fiftieth anniversary of his conversion, for example, Turner planned to return to Abbeville for a weeklong retreat so that he could roam over its hills and through its woods, recalling the youthful spiritual experiences that had proved to be such a profound source of meaning and orientation for him throughout his long life.[79]

Conclusion

The culture of Upcountry black Methodist preachers was primarily an oral one, backed by an extensive use of memorization. Some black preachers, like Turner, were able to read the Bible, but even they relied extensively on memory. The African-derived practice of relying upon memory in order to obtain freedom from texts strengthened their preaching in many ways. Unencumbered by texts, these orators delivered sermons that were characterized by remarkable power, fluidity, and virtuosity. Their sermons were not dry or pretentious, as the efforts of more intellectual preachers often were. According to students of the black preaching tradition, the intense personal, experiential, and narrative emphases employed in Cook's sermon have long been characteristic of black preaching styles.

Clearly, some white preachers sought to learn from black preachers' sermonic excellence. It is difficult to believe that what happened between Uncle Toliver and William Parks on a formal basis was not replicated in informal ways many times throughout the southern states. African-influenced preaching styles were apparently more acceptable to white Upcountry residents than were African-influenced audience responses, such as shouting. In any case, both black preaching and shouting were better appreciated or tolerated by white South Carolinians during the summer camp meetings held outdoors.

We should inquire about the shortcomings, as well as the strengths, of a preaching style based so thoroughly on orality and memory. For one thing, we are deprived of the mature self-reflections of most Upcountry preachers. The fragmentary data we do have were set down by literate observers—at best, by participants like Turner who bridged the oral and literate cultures. Also, many of these preachers held the modern world at arm's length. The sermons by Brown and Jasper (on God's commanding the sun to stand still) threw down a challenge to a society that had largely accepted the findings of Copernicus and Galileo. But most listeners, black and white, apparently considered tolerating such an outdated stance a small price to pay for hearing good preaching. In any event, the future of black ministry seemed to belong not so much to preachers resembling Cook or Porter but to those, like Turner, who were capable of operating with equal confidence in both the Euro-American and African American worlds and could masterfully blend the influences of both in their preaching. Still, while few black Methodist ministers during the days of slavery possessed all of the advantages that Turner did, most were able to provide the community leadership needed for a new era. They provided a strong strain of continuity during a period of rapid change.

The lives of Cook, Porter, and Turner help to demonstrate the range of opportunities in religious leadership that existed for black Americans during slavery days in the South Carolina Upcountry (and adjacent regions such as Georgia). In some southern cities and towns, friendly reciprocity between whites and blacks was at least as important a feature of interracial religious interactions as were subordination and repression of blacks. Certain whites such as Fair, as well as blacks such as Porter, assailed and disobeyed the egregious laws in the slave states against teaching blacks to read and write; and in the South's cities and towns, public opinion among whites and blacks often favored their actions. In his later years Turner emphasized his youthful friendships with both whites and blacks and the acceptability of his ministry among people of both races. However, even the sense of common striving for salvation through the same Jesus, which often shaped religious interactions in the antebellum urban South, could not fundamentally alter the cruelties and paradoxes that underlay slavery and the South's racial caste system. The slave preacher William aspired to much the same goal of ministerial leadership Henry Turner did, but one was barbarously killed while the other received nurturance from some blacks and whites. In the end, even Turner felt compelled to leave the South before the conflict over slavery reached its bloody climax in civil war.

Notes

I wish to thank Professor Ronald N. Liburd of Florida A & M University for reading this article and making helpful suggestions for revision.

1. *Voice of Missions*, February 1897.

2. Building on James Weldon Johnson's classic *God's Trombones: Seven Negro Sermons in Verse* (New York: Viking, 1927) have been such works as: Eugene Genovese, *Roll, Jordan, Roll: The World the Slaves Made* (New York: Vintage, 1976), 255–79; Albert Raboteau, *Slave Religion: The "Invisible Institution" in the Antebellum South* (New York: Oxford University Press, 1978), 135–37, 231–39; and for Baptists, Mechal Sobel, *Trabelin' On: The Slave Journey to an Afro-Baptist Faith* (Westport, Conn.: Greenwood Press, 1979), 185–200, 235–42; Walter F. Pitts, *Old Ship of Zion: The Afro-Baptist Ritual in the African Diaspora* (New York: Oxford University Press, 1993). John B. Boles has shown that historians have neglected much evidence of biracial interactions in antebellum southern religion in "The Discovery of Southern Religious History," in *Interpreting Southern History*, Boles and Evelyn T. Nolen, eds. (Baton Rouge: Louisiana State University Press, 1987), 518–19; see also Boles, ed., *Masters and Slaves in the House of the Lord: Race and Religion in the American South, 1740–1870* (Lexington: University Press of Kentucky, 1988). On antebellum black Methodism in the South Carolina Upcountry, see Stephen Ward Angell, *Bishop Henry McNeal Turner and African-American Religion in the South* (Knoxville: University of Tennessee Press, 1992), 10–23; and Janet Duitsman Cornelius, *"When I Can Read My Title Clear": Literacy, Slavery, and Religion in the Antebellum South* (Columbia: University of South Carolina Press, 1991), 34–58. Nancy Ashmore Cooper gives an interesting sketch of James R. Rosemond, who ministered for thirty-six years as a slave and is credited with organizing fifty Upcountry Methodist churches. "Where Everybody is Somebody: African-American Churches in South Carolina," in Charles H. Lippy, ed., *Religion in South Carolina* (Columbia: University of South Carolina Press, 1993), 128.
3. George P. Rawick, *The American Slave: A Composite Autobiography* (Westport, Conn.: Greenwood Press, 1972), vol. II, pt. i, 118–19. See Genovese, *Roll, Jordan, Roll*, 258.
4. *Christian Recorder*, November 24, 1866.
5. *Christian Recorder*, January 20, 1866.
6. Reginald F. Hildebrand, "Methodist Episcopal Policy on the Ordination of Black Ministers, 1784–1864," *Methodist History* 20 (1982): 124–41.
7. On the connections of Charleston's black Methodists to the Vesey revolt, see Vincent Harding, "Religion and Resistance among Antebellum Negroes, 1800–1860," in August Meier and Elliott Rudwick, eds., *The Making of Black America* (New York: Atheneum, 1969), I, 184–87. The later development of Charleston's black Methodism is discussed in Erskine Clarke, *Wrestlin' Jacob: A Portrait of Religion in the Old South* (Atlanta: John Knox Press, 1979), 83–158. The establishment of the AME Church in the Upcountry is discussed in Abram Weston, "How African Methodism Was Introduced in the Upcountry," in Benjamin Arnett, ed., *Proceedings of the Quarto-Centennial of the African ME Church of South Carolina* (Charleston, 1890).
8. "Bishop Turner's Plain Talk," *Christian Recorder*, September 23, 1886; *Voice of Missions*, February 1897.
9. Abram Weston, "How African Methodism Was Introduced in the Upcountry," 71.

10. Quoted in Raboteau, *Slave Religion*, 236.

11. *Christian Recorder*, December 15, 1866.

12. Theophilus G. Steward, *Fifty Years in the Gospel Ministry* (Philadelphia, 1921), 71–72.

13. *Christian Recorder*, September 23, 1886: reference to Murphy as "black as ink," July 17, 1890.

14. Henry H. Mitchell, *The Recovery of Preaching* (San Francisco: Harper and Row, 1977), 20–21.

15. Rawick, *American Slave*, vol. II, pt. i, 224.

16. *Ibid.*, vol. III, pt. iii, 169.

17. *Ibid.*, vol. II, pt. i, 323; vol. III, pt. iv, 250; Genovese, *Roll, Jordan, Roll*, 262.

18. *With Head and Heart: The Autobiography of Howard Thurman* (San Diego: Harcourt Brace Jovanovich, 1979), 16–17.

19. Testimony of Major Nelson in John W. Blassingame, *Slave Testimony: Two Centuries of Letters, Speeches, Interviews and Autobiographies* (Baton Rouge: Louisiana State University Press, 1977), 497.

20. Rawick, *American Slave*, vol. III, pt. iv, 52.

21. Ibid., vol. II, pt. i, 231.

22. Rosser H. Taylor, "The Church and its Auxiliaries," in Ernest M. Lander Jr. and Robert K. Ackerman, eds., *Perspectives in South Carolina History: The First 300 Years* (Columbia: University of South Carolina Press, 1973), 124.

23. Dickson Bruce, *And They All Sang Hallelujah: Plain-Folk Camp-Meeting Religion, 1800–1845* (Knoxville: University of Tennessee Press, 1974), 74–75.

24. William P. Harrison, *The Gospel among the Slaves* (Nashville, 1893), 380; "Luther," "Two Negro Preachers I Have Heard," *Southern Christian Advocate*, November 24, 1887.

25. Rawick, *American Slave*, vol. II, pt. ii, 111; see Sarah Fitzpatrick, quoted in Blassingame, *Slave Testimony*, 642–43.

26. *Christian Recorder*, July 17, 1890.

27. Rawick, *American Slave*, vol. III, pt. iii, 19.

28. Abundant evidence of the existence of these kinds of connections, however, has been assembled by Sterling Stuckey, *Slave Culture: Nationalist Theory and the Foundations of Black America* (New York: Oxford University Press, 1987), 3–97.

29. *Voice of Missions*, February 1897.

30. In Roper's letter, the preacher is named George, not William. Letter from Moses Roper to Thomas Price, June 27, 1836, in Blassingame, *Slave Testimony*, 24–25; *Columbia Telescope*, May 23, 1825, quoted in Lowry Ware, "The Burning of Jerry: The Last Slave Execution by Fire in South Carolina?" *South Carolina Historical Magazine* 91 (April 1990): 101–2.

31. *Christian Recorder*, September 29, 1866.

32. *Southern Christian Advocate*, October 23, 1873.

33. Henry M. Turner, "Wayside Dots and Jots," *Christian Recorder*, January 8, 1880; Alexander W. Wayman, *Cyclopaedia of African Methodism* (Baltimore, 1882), 41.

34. *Southern Christian Advocate,* November 24, 1887.
35. *Christian Recorder,* January 8, 1880.
36. *Southern Christian Advocate,* November 24, 1887.
37. James H. Evans, *We Have Been Believers: An African-American Systematic Theology* (Minneapolis: Fortress Press, 1992), 50.
38. Compare Cook's sermon to "The Prodigal Son" in Johnson, *God's Trombones,* 21–25.
39. Mitchell, *The Recovery of Preaching,* 32.
40. *Southern Christian Advocate,* November 24, 1887.
41. *Christian Recorder,* January 8, 1880; Mary Veals in Rawick, *American Slave,* vol. III, pt. iv, 167–69; Wayman, *Cyclopaedia,* 41.
42. Robert L. Hall, "Black and White Christians in Florida," in Boles, *Masters and Slaves,* 83.
43. *Christian Recorder,* January 8, 1880.
44. Johnson, *God's Trombones,* 5.
45. Turner, "In Memoriam," *Voice of Missions,* November 1895.
46. Ibid.; "Talk with Bishop Turner: What He Says of the Affair at Palmetto," undated newspaper clipping ca. May 1899, Manuscript Department, Moorland-Springarn Research Center, Howard University.
47. Edmund Drago, *Black Politicians and Reconstruction in Georgia: A Splendid Failure* (Baton Rouge: Louisiana State University Press, 1982), 38–39, 97–98; Robert E. Perdue, *The Negro in Savannah, 1865–1900* (New York: Exposition Press, 1973), 47–48; John W. Blassingame, "Before the Ghetto: The Making of the Black Community in Savannah, Georgia," *Journal of Social History* 6 (1973): 477–80.
48. *Voice of Missions,* November 1895; Wayman, *Cyclopaedia,* 129.
49. *Memorial Services: Tribute to the Honorable Charles Sumner, Held in St. Phillips A.M.E. Church, Savannah, Georgia, March 18, 1874* (Savannah, 1874), 4.
50. *Voice of Missions,* November 1895.
51. "Wealthiest of the colored families:" *Christian Recorder,* July 12, 1888; Angell, *Bishop Henry McNeal Turner,* 7–10.
52. William J. Simmons, *Men of Mark: Eminent, Progressive, and Rising* (New York: Arno Press, 1968), 807–9; *Harper's Weekly,* December 12, 1863.
53. *Memorial Services: Tribute to Charles Sumner,* 12.
54. Fair's paper to the Bible Society: Cornelius, *"When I Can Read My Title Clear,"* 138–39; Turner's instruction by lawyers: Simmons, *Men of Mark,* 810. Fair's close acquaintance with Turner is demonstrated by his 1854 endorsement of Turner's ministry. Then Fair stated that he had known Turner "for many years" (see the *Atlanta Constitution,* May 16, 1915, 11A).
55. In the *Voice of Missions,* Feburary 1897, Henry McNeal Turner eulogized a white Presbyterian minister who had served an Abbeville church when Henry Turner was a boy. The minister's name was Daniel McNeal Turner, and while Henry Turner does not in the article acknowledge a blood relationship, it does not seem farfetched to suggest, on the basis of name similarity, that there probably was one.

56. Rawick, *American Slave*, vol. II, pt. i, 193.

57. See Glenn T. Eskew, "Black Elitism and the Failure of Paternalism in Post-bellum Georgia: The Case of Bishop Lucius Henry Holsey," *Journal of Southern History* 58 (November 1992): 644–45, 653–57.

58. *Christian Recorder*, January 20, 1866.

59. *Voice of Missions*, August 1895.

60. *Voice of Missions*, February 1899.

61. Harrison, *Gospel among the Slaves*, 379–80; for Alonzo Johnson's comments on seekin' the Lord, see his essay "Pray's House Spirit" in this volume.

62. For more information on his evangelistic experiences in Macon and Athens, Georgia, and New Orleans, see Angell, *Bishop Henry McNeal Turner*, 23–30. Turner's prayer meetings among slaves and the extent of his reading, *National Cyclopedia of American Biography*, s.v. "Turner, Henry McNeal"; Turner "a white man galvanized," Benjamin Tanner, *An Apology for African Methodism* (Baltimore, 1867), 416; Turner "a Negro Spurgeon," *Christian Recorder*, April 9, 1885; Turner proves his ability to preach extemporaneously, Robert Anderson, *The Life of Robert Anderson* (Macon, Ga., 1892), 24–25; "friendly relations . . . between whites and blacks," "Talk with Bishop Turner." See n. 46.

63. Edwin S. Redkey, ed., *Respect Black: The Writings and Speeches of Henry McNeal Turner* (New York: Arno Press, 1971), 11.

64. *Macon American Union*, February 26, 1869.

65. *Christian Recorder*, March 22, 1862.

66. *Memorial Services: Tribute to the Honorable Charles Sumner*, 11.

67. *Christian Recorder*, July 12, 1862.

68. Angell, *Bishop Henry McNeal Turner*, 30–59.

69. It is beyond the scope of this essay to detail Turner's various careers as Reconstruction era politician, civil rights activist, black theologian, supporter of women's ordination to the ministry, and advocate of African missions and emigration. For information on these aspects of his life, see Angell, *Bishop Henry McNeal Turner*, 60–274.

70. *Christian Recorder*, July 1, 1865; November 24, 1866.

71. "Laudable Ambition," *Christian Recorder*, October 21, 1875; "must be crazy," *Voice of Missions*, December 1893; Columbia revival, *Christian Recorder*, September 23, October 7, 1875; "preach till men fear," see Henry M. Turner, *The Genius and Theory of Methodist Polity: or the Machinery of Methodism Practically Illustrated Through a Series of Questions and Answers*, 2d rev. ed. (Philadelphia, 1889), 113–14, 226–27, 232.

72. Daniel Payne, *Recollections of Seventy Years* (New York: Arno Press, 1969; originally published in 1886), 253–54.

73. Turner, "Introduction," *The Hymn Book of the African Methodist Episcopal Church* (Philadelphia, 1883), iv; *Voice of Missions*, December 1897.

74. Payne, *Recollections*, 275.

75. From 1865 to 1872 Turner lived in Macon; from 1872 to about 1880, in Savannah; from 1880 until his death, in 1915, in Atlanta.

76. *Voice of Missions*, September 1895.

77. On Turner's African emigrationism, see Edwin S. Redkey, *Black Exodus: Black Nationalist and Back-to-Africa Movements* (New Haven: Yale University Press, 1969). On his family's outlook toward Africa, see Redkey, *Respect Black*, 125; *Christian Recorder*, July 25, 1889; October 22, 1891.

78. Tanner, *Apology*, 415. Tanner would have had in mind the eccentric Bishop Payne. Probably he was also comparing Turner to South Carolina's white secessionist politicians.

79. *Voice of Missions*, February 1899.

Biblical Interpretation, Ecclesiology, and Black Southern Religious Leaders, 1860–1920

A Case Study of AMEZ Bishop James Walker Hood

Sandy Dwayne Martin

One of the most fascinating black religious and political leaders in the South between 1860 and 1920 is James Walker Hood (1831–1918). Hood's public career indeed was momentous in both religious and political worlds. Born in the southeastern section of Pennsylvania to free parents in 1831, Hood grew up as a member of the Union Church of Africans, a group that was founded in the early 1800s by Peter Spencer but has been confined mainly to the middle Atlantic states. In the 1850s Hood journeyed to New York City; entered the ministry; affiliated with the African Methodist Episcopal Zion Church (AMEZ, or Zion); pastored in New England; became a missionary to Nova Scotia during the early 1860s; returned to pastor in Bridgeport, Connecticut, in 1863; and left for North Carolina in the winter of 1864 to minister among the newly freed people. He also became a great organizer for the AMEZ Church in North Carolina, Virginia, and South Carolina.

During the 1860s Hood participated in Reconstruction activities in North Carolina, serving as a delegate to the state Constitutional Convention from 1867 to 1868, as assistant superintendent for education in the state, as an officer for educational matters in the Freedmen's Bureau, and, briefly, as a magistrate. He helped to establish what is now Fayetteville State University and the AMEZ denominational school Livingstone College, located in Salisbury, North Carolina. Furthermore, he played a leading role in establishing the major denominational newspaper, *The Star of Zion*. His prominence in both the political and religious worlds helped to propel him into the AMEZ episcopacy in 1872. Hood served as active bishop until 1916, forty-four years, half of that time as senior bishop. The

Zion prelate published five books (two books of sermons, a commentary on the biblical book of Revelation, and two histories of the AMEZ Church) along with numerous articles in the *AMEZ Quarterly Review*, the *Star of Zion*, and other contemporary sources. Undoubtedly, this Zion minister and bishop left a profound imprint on southern black religious life.

This essay explores Hood's career as a religious leader, focusing particularly upon his understanding of the nature and purpose of the church (ecclesiology) and the manner in which he responded to a number of ideas that challenged some of the traditional tenets of Christianity, and pays special attention to his understanding of the Bible regarding the latter. The basic thesis of the following pages is that Hood appropriated the meaning of the nature and purpose of the church to encompass his concern for the African American community, and that his embrace of traditional Christian doctrines and biblical interpretations was undergirded by his fervent commitment to liberating his race. Examining these ideas of Hood is of immense importance since he represents the mainline, mainstream black denominational leaders operating in the South from the Civil War to World War I. Though he remained throughout his life a political adviser to African Americans, Hood's primary commitment was to the church. But like most of the denominational leaders during this era, the Zion leader did not make an absolute division between the sacred and the secular. His efforts to build up the Zion denomination and to spread the Gospel reflected both temporal and spiritual concerns for his racial siblings. Furthermore, his political stances fell between the "radicalism" of Henry McNeal Turner, with an emphasis upon racial emigration and support for the Democratic Party in later years, and Booker T. Washington, who appears to have been too quiescent regarding the adversities inflicted on southern blacks, such as lynching and disfranchisement. Hood was conservative, or moderate, in his approach, seeking to form alliances with sympathetic whites; but he stood firmly against disfranchisement and segregation, and he deplored lawless acts against blacks.

Thus we may explore Hood's ecclesiological and biblical views in the following pages as a prism through which to understand the black denominational leadership in the South during the period 1860–1920. On one hand, the reader should discover a uniqueness and particularity of black Christians' approaches to the church and the world. On the other hand, this essay should clearly demonstrate how integrally connected and interrelated were black and white forms of American Christianity, especially southern Protestantism, during this period. It is important to understand Hood as a southern religious leader. Though reaching maturity in the Northeast, he spent fifty-four of his eighty-seven years as a resident of North Carolina, establishing his religious, economic, familial, and political roots permanently in Fayetteville, while as bishop he canvassed the country carrying out his episcopal duties.

Hood's Ecclesiology and the Black Experience

Consistent with most Methodists, other Protestants, and mainline Christians of the time, Hood envisioned the Christian religion as the one true religion revealed by God to humanity. It was incumbent upon the church in general and individuals in particular to do their respective shares in spreading the faith. Hood was firmly convinced that Christianity ensured its adherents of eternal life, happiness, and bliss. But he also believed that the spread of Christian principles liberated societies from backwardness and corruption, making the social order a blessing for the community at large. In addition, an 1899 article revealed that Hood was consistent with his Wesleyan or Methodist tradition in that he believed Christianity brought temporal benefits to the individual in the present.[1] For example, Hood concludes his article "The Character and the Persuasive Power of the Christian Religion," in a 1904 *Quarterly Review* issue, by stating, "We are persuaded to embrace the Christian [religion] because it secures to mortal beings that which cannot be obtained by any other means; viz, present and eternal happiness. The Apostle Paul tells us that goodness is profitable unto all things, having the promise of the life that now is and that which is to come." In addition, Hood had stated earlier in the article that the Christian religion is not contrary to true reason, contrary to the claims of those whom he regarded as skeptics and infidels.[2]

An enlightening look at Hood's ecclesiology or views of the church, particularly as it relates to the black experience in the United States, may be gained from exploring part three of his 1914 *Sketch of the Early History of the AMEZ Church*, titled "God's Purpose in the Negro Church as Seen in the History of the Movement." Published four years before his death, this piece undoubtedly represents the mature thought of the senior bishop of the Zion Methodists.[3] This section is both a history of the early black church and an apologia for black independent denominations. In discussing the origins of the black church, Hood makes the point that he is analyzing not simply the history of one denomination of black Christians but a whole movement of independent denominations. He makes it clear that the black church (that is, the family of independent black denominations) arose during the late eighteenth and early nineteenth centuries because of unambiguous racial prejudice. By segregating seating and such ceremonies as the Lord's Supper and baptism, many whites made it quite clear that blacks were not welcomed as equal spiritual siblings in the churches. As a result, black churches in various places began almost simultaneously an exodus to form independent communities.

It is interesting and significant that Hood leaves aside the debate that had raged for decades between the AME (the African Methodist Episcopal Church, founded in 1816) and the Zionites concerning which of them constituted the first independent black denomination. In the past this had been a major point of contention between the two groups, especially during the era prior to 1848, when the AMEZ had not yet affixed Zion to its official name, thus occasioning a great deal of confusion in the minds of many as to the respective identities of the two bodies. This debate over the question of which of the two had historical priority was generated by a combination of concerns. First, there was an honest difference of opinion as to which actually premiered. Each seemed to have insisted upon pushing its denominational origins back to the earliest emergence of its first independent congregation while tending to place the formation of its rival with the date of its absolute, connectional independence from the white-controlled Methodist Episcopal Church. Second, the members of black congregations would have considered it an honor to be the oldest black denomination, so they competed for the distinction. Third, black and white Methodists despised schism and encouraged ecumenicity. The group that appeared second (and essentially for the same reasons as the first group) would have the burden of explaining why it did not unite with the first into one stronger black denomination for reasons of racial and religious unity.

But Hood's purpose is more sweeping than a mere denominational controversy over institutional priority, he insists. What he strives to put forth is that there was a *racial* movement happening simultaneously. Implicitly, it mattered little which denomination preceded the others by ten or twenty or thirty years. In the grand panorama of time and ecclesiastical worldview, they all occurred rather simultaneously. He writes:

> The colored members of the different Christian denominations, of one accord, in all parts of the country, and as nearly as can now be learned, at about the same time, separated from the whites, and formed each for themselves, a church of the same faith and order, as those from which they separated, leaving the white churches almost without a colored membership.[4]

This last clause is not accurate, at least not for the Methodists. Actually, more blacks remained with the white-controlled Methodist Episcopal churches than removed themselves. But Hood's basic thesis is more intriguing and is fundamentally accurate: the churches should not interpret these occurrences, separation from white-controlled groups, as specific de-

nominational phenomena but as representations of a general movement
for racial independence. According to Hood,

> To our mind, this was not an Episcopalian, Presbyterian or Bap-
> tist movement. It was not a Bethel [AME], Union [Union Church of
> Africans founded as separate denomination in 1813], nor Zion
> [AMEZ] movement, but a general, grand, united and simultaneous
> Negro movement. It was the race that was oppressed, and it was the
> race that moved.
>
> It was a movement by which a race, hampered, proscribed, regu-
> lated and oppressed, gave a grand and united exhibition of its deter-
> mination to find in its organizations that religious liberty which was
> denied it in the white church.[5]

Hood's innovative and creative argument could be simply the insight
of a careful observer; or it could be influenced greatly by the fact that
blacks, during an age of increased racial indifference, hostility, and discrimination, needed to look beyond the particularities of their differences
and focus upon the universe of their common experiences. At any rate,
Hood's thesis is a master stroke in terms of historiography, ecumenicity,
and efforts to achieve racial harmony and cooperation.

But Hood's ruminations on African American religious history go beyond this insightful interpretation. Black Christians generally during this
period interpreted the Civil War, the resulting emancipation of African
American enslaved people, and the subsequent achievement of citizenship rights and new economic opportunity as God's divine action in
human history working through what were often very imperfect earthly
instrumentalities. In other words, they identified the war, emancipation,
and enfranchisement as a modern-day Exodus akin to that recorded in the
Old Testament or Hebrew Scriptures. But Hood offered a new version of
the modern Exodus. It is not that he downplayed the significance of racial
freedom as a result of the Civil War, but, for the Zion bishop, the late-
eighteenth- and early-nineteenth-century emergence of independent
black denominations was not simply one of many dramas in human history. Rather, this exodus of blacks from white-controlled churches was
paralleled in momentousness only by the Exodus event itself, when God
liberated the enslaved, oppressed Hebrews from bondage in Pharaoh's
Egypt. At Mother Zion Church in New York City, October 1896, nearly
twenty years before the publication of *Sketch*, Hood elaborated upon this
idea in a sermon based upon Deuteronomy 32:11–12 and Psalms 149:2.
This is obviously a motif that he had reflected upon and repeated over a
period of at least twenty years. According to Hood,

The coming out of the colored people from the white church of America, and their being formed into a separate organization, *is the only event in the world's history which bears any resemblance to this deliverance of the children of Israel from Egyptian bondage and their formation into "a peculiar people."* Why did the Israelites come out of Egypt? Because they were oppressed. Why did the black people come out from the white church? Because they were oppressed;—at least this is what is seen on the surface (italics added)[6]

The bishop was certainly sounding a recurring theme in African American general and religious history, that black people in some significant sense were a chosen people. But he was also advancing an interpretation that theologians of black liberation operating in the final decade of the twentieth century found historically fruitful for the development of their idea that God identifies with and works through the oppressed in society. Hood specifically placed the black church at the very heart of God's liberating activity in the world. While many leaders might differ with Hood as to which was the modern-day Exodus experience for blacks—emancipation or the rise of independent black denominations—nearly all would agree with Hood's understanding of the providential nature and mission of the black church as the key instrument for the liberation of African Americans and the black race. Hood claimed that the collective and paralleled actions of black Christian groups' seceding from white-controlled denominations were not mere organizational schisms. According to the account in *Sketch,* this coerced departure of blacks (because they clearly could not remain in such inhospitable and uncharitable environments) actually fit into the divine plan of God relative to developing the black race.

First, the black church was one of the "powerful instrumentalities by which slavery was overthrown"[7] with its support of the underground railroad and by providing the forum from which abolitionists could agitate against the slave system. Second, the black church was God's instrument in other areas of human enhancement. The Christian ministry represented one among the few areas in which pre-Civil War blacks could practice some form of leadership and development. For example, the noble and great abolitionist Frederick Douglass had his start as a public speaker in the Zion church, having gained his leadership skills by serving in the capacities of "sexton, class-leader, and local preacher." The church was indispensable for the entire race. "It was his [the black person's] common school, his lyceum, his college, his municipal counsel, his legislative hall and his congress,"[8] an observation mirrored by many late-twentieth-century students of black general and religious history. The heavy partici-

pation of black *ministers* in civic affairs during the Reconstruction era
caused dismay for some, wrote Hood. But there were few "intelligent
leaders" besides the Christian minister who could labor on behalf of the
race.

As late as 1914 Hood was still speaking of the black church as an
effective avenue by which the black race could lift itself. Blacks required
an institution like the black church through which they could develop
their talents. Hood, by implication, held no confidence in the idea that
whites would overlook color and invite blacks into their circles on a plane
of equality. He was not naive about racial prejudice. He wrote:

> To reach the top, the black man must go up on his own
> plane—he must climb his own ladder. The white man will never
> step aside to make way for him. The feeling of superiority is inher-
> ent in the white race in this country. We certainly are giving out no
> secrets now; nor will any white man charge us with slander or feel
> offended, for he boasts of his superiority. We do not admit it; we
> deny it, but he claims it.[9]

Therefore, Hood argued, blacks should entertain no hopes that
whites would take it upon themselves to lift blacks to a position equal
with them. But "when the black man on his own merit and on his own
ladder has reached the top, there are many who will grasp his hand in
recognition and even in congratulation, because they don't have to stoop
down to reach his hand." Hood was undoubtedly speaking from general
observation and autobiographical experience. The example he used to
portray the manner in which the black church provides black persons the
opportunity to uplift themselves is the respect accorded to black bishops
by white Methodists. In many instances, says Hood, black bishops were
requested to preach in white churches while other black ministers of equal
talents were shut out. The black church had provided these persons the
opportunity to attain the status of bishop. And if they conducted themselves well in the opportunities presented, those black bishops or leaders,
by demonstrating the capacities of the black race, could pave the way for
others.[10] Thus ecclesiastical independence of black Christians benefited
the black individual as well as the entire race.

Hood's View of the Ministry and
Its Place in the African American Community

Consistent with Methodist doctrine and discipline and with the expectations of Christianity in general during this era, Hood set a high standard for ministers of the Gospel. In 1876, four years after he was elevated

to the office of bishop and during a time in which Reconstruction was winding down throughout the South, Hood exhorted his North Carolinian ministers upon the meaning and characteristics of the Christian ministry. He insisted upon "a pure ministry," one not only free of "scandalous crimes" but one that also avoided even "the appearance of evil." No matter how talented, educated, or energetic one might be, one must be morally pure. Indeed, Hood embraced the principles of the holiness movement found in many Methodist churches during this era (for example, it was the duty of the Christian to strive with the help of God to attain during this present life a state of Christian perfection, freedom from all known sin). He encouraged the proper authorities in the church to see that ministers were carefully supervised; that mistakes and weaknesses were addressed; and if the person persisted in living contrary to the way of holiness, that that person be expelled.[11]

Ministers *were* actually expelled from time to time for behavior deemed unbecoming of a Christian or minister. The minutes of the Central North Carolina Conference meeting in its third session, held in Statesville, November 22–27, 1882, reveal an interesting look at the discipline that Hood, other bishops, and the conferences enforced, sometimes resulting in expulsions. In counseling "moral purity," Hood noted that few people actually had bad reputations. The majority of Zion ministers appeared to be morally upright, and Hood noted that fewer cases of immorality surfaced at that time than had surfaced more than five years earlier. The prelate wondered if more ministers were living better lives or if some had become more adept at hiding their improprieties. Hood named the moral ills affecting the denomination: licentiousness, intemperance, and adultery. He stated that no one should be shocked that he would suggest such spiritual maladies existed within the conference. From the pages of the minutes, Hood observed that twenty persons had been expelled for adultery, and some of these individuals now ministered "in other denominations." Hood also claimed that an approximate number of individuals had been ousted because of alcoholic intemperance. It is not clear whether he referred to the minutes of the Central North Carolina Conference, both the North Carolina Conference and the Central North Carolina Conference, or the entire connection. Nor do I have sufficient information to tell whether adultery in any or all of these cases was understood solely as the very act of illicit sex, maybe including fornication as well, or whether "appearances" of impropriety in sexual matters also were sufficient to be judged guilty of the sin. At any rate, it is clear that the denomination and Hood enforced strict discipline. Some would remind the stricter disciplinarians that the New Testament, and presumably the words of Jesus, counseled that the tares should be allowed to grow with the wheat until the angels of God at the end of the Age separated them. Hood replied that the tares and wheat could grow together, but when the tares ripened then they should be gotten rid of.[12] Although the specific charges leveled against the alleged offender are unclear, an example of expulsion occurred when the Committee on Investigation brought back an adverse report on a Reverend D. L. Johnson at the 1899 North Carolina Conference held in Kinston. "Report was received and Bro. D. L. Johnson was expelled."[13]

As prelate and presiding officer at annual conferences, Hood could show mercy, leniency, and understanding toward offending ministers. At the 1881 Central North Carolina Conference in Charlotte, a Reverend Henry Williams desired to be received back into the conference.[14] Two years prior he had left the Zion connection to affiliate with the AME, the chief rivals of the Zionites. Apparently Williams had left with some rather harsh words against Hood and some other members of the conference. At the current conference, Williams apologized to Hood and the other members, but an R. S. Rieves seemed to have been left unsatisfied. He believed that satisfaction should be rendered to a church in Cumberland County, supposedly a church with which Williams had been connected in some fashion. Interestingly, Hood stated that Williams's contrition was sufficient. The recorder of the session noted the response of Hood. "Furthermore, [Hood said] that he did not care what a man might say about him (the bishop) if he love Zion; and if any man among us wanted to go to Bethel, he would lend him to that church long enough to convince himself, as Brother Williams had been convinced." In a related matter, the Reverend A. F. Goslin seems to have denied that the quarterly conference at Statesville had the legal right to recommend readmitting Williams to the conference. Again, Hood took a lenient approach and declared that the quarterly conference's action was indeed legal.[15]

The above episode is significant for a number of reasons. First, it demonstrates that Hood was a compassionate and, in the context of the times, understanding and forgiving episcopal officer. Second, this event reveals that in the post–Civil War South and throughout the nation, ministers frequently moved from one connection to the other among the four contending Methodist forces at the time: the CME, the Methodist Episcopal (North), the AME, and the AMEZ. Sometimes these individuals came to regret their actions and returned to their original denominations. Third, Hood was aware that there was indeed fierce competition for ministers among the Methodist bodies in the South. Williams's return had authenticated for many Zionites that their denomination was superior to the AME. With the need for good, hardworking ministers, why deny or discourage an individual's return to the denomination at the risk of losing his services to a rival group? Finally, this and other episodes demonstrate that black leaders and church members held high standards of moral conduct.

Some individuals regarded Hood's judicial fairness and mercy as signs of weakness or lack of will in dealing forthrightly with the guilty. Hood noted this perception of his style in the 1876 North Carolina Conference. This, the bishop pointedly stated, was a misjudgment of the man. Of course he would stand on the side of fairness for moral as well as practical reasons:

> What of the M. E. Church with its millions of money ready to buy every dissatisfied man, be his character what it may? The M. E. Church South ready to receive and turn over to the little body of colored members it has organized [the Christian Methodist Episcopal Church] all who have any grievances? Then the Bethel [AME] connection constantly misrepresenting us, we have need to be precise in dealing with our members, that none have occasion to complain of unfairness.[16]

But Hood would adopt stringent measures and positions if he thought the integrity of the ministry, the denomination, and the Christian faith demanded it. At the same 1881 Central North Carolina Conference where Hood paved the way for an easier return of a former minister, he denied the admission of another. A Presbyterian minister, Felix Thompson, then a student of Biddle University (now Johnson C. Smith University) in Charlotte, desired to leave the Presbyterian Church and affiliate with the Zionites. After reading his letter of recommendation from the Reverend S. Mattoon, the president of the university, Hood issued a ruling that was sustained by the conference. Hood found the letter inadequate. The bishop stated that it talked about character but did not constitute a clear, unambiguous recommendation for admission. Interestingly, shortly thereafter Reverend Mattoon entered the conference, was seated, and just before adjournment was invited to make remarks. He complimented the work of the *Star of Zion* and the progress of the Zion annual conference. He also discussed the work of Biddle University, but he said nothing of Thompson.[17] Perhaps Mattoon was unaware of the adverse action that had already transpired; had he known, he might have addressed himself in clearer supportive terms for Thompson's application. It is also possible that the president knew that his letter would not be sufficient and had purposefully written it in such a manner to refuse politely an endorsement of Thompson's candidacy. Finally, it is quite possible that subsequently the whole matter was cleared up, that Mattoon made the necessary literary changes or gave sufficient verbal support in Thompson's favor. The significance of the episode lay in the fact that the Zion denomination, and Hood in particular, insisted on the highest standards in the connection's ministry and that it was willing to expel, readmit, or refuse to admit, in accordance with those standards.

In an exhortation to the members of the 1884 Kentucky Annual Conference, Hood also pointed out the evils to be avoided and the traits to be cultivated among those who were shepherds of God's people.[18] Ministers must avoid selfishness and self-indulgence. A pastor had the obligation to know each member of the parish and visit each person monthly. He should not devote an inordinate amount of time to "good looking members (some of whom are fast in mischief and loose in habit)," while neglecting those church members who are ill. Ministers, of course, should avoid the shameful use of alcohol as a beverage and shun the pitiful habit of tobacco use. In this episcopal address, Hood, significantly, warned ministers that they should not become overly involved in political matters that would separate them from the fidelity to their ministry, since the ministry demanded all of one's time. According to Hood, ministers "have the same right to vote, and to freely express their political opinions that other people have, and if those in their charge want any political information which they possess it is their duty to give it, and they ought to inform themselves as far as is convenient on all public matters. The priests lips should dispense knowledge, but they have not the time to play the politician."[19] In other words, the minister must avoid the role of a politician but should remain a valuable repository of political and civic knowledge for the benefit of his people, not to further personal political ambitions.

Given Hood's crucial involvement in the convention of North Carolina black leaders in 1865, the Reconstruction State Convention of 1867–68, his campaign to have the constitution ratified by the state voters, and his participation in the politics of the Republican Party, it might appear incongruent or hypocritical at first glance for Hood to have expressed concern about ministers' involvements in political affairs. And to some extent it was. It must be noted, however, that Hood counseled not political quiescence but a *vocational* devotion to ministerial duties because they require all of one's time. Second, the bishop might also have defended his earlier political activities as necessitated by the circumstances of the time. He noted in his 1895 history of Zion that "the few colored ministers who came South during or soon after the war were the only well-informed leaders the people had, and, whatever [their] inclination, they were, at that period, compelled at times to accept positions as representatives to prevent the people from being misrepresented by men too ignorant to do them credit."[20] Third, people must not be misled to believe that an undue number of African American ministers participated in politics, according to the bishop. Hood claimed that "within the range of our observation not one in twenty have been active politicians."[21] These statements are essentially correct. But those ministers who at the time of Hood's exhortation desired political participation did in fact have forerunners who entered politics because of their personal and racial desires, not necessarily because they were the only qualified spokespersons for the race at the time. Also, the perception of the number of minister-politicians might have been exaggerated, but they constituted a great proportion of black officeholders and activists.

There is a fourth reason Hood would have considered his admonition for ministers to avoid politics as not hypocritical or inconsistent with his own political record. Somewhat surprisingly, he never saw himself as a politician but as a minister of God carrying out the work of building the Kingdom upon earth. Hood was offered a political appointment to serve as Collector of Customs for the Port of Wilmington, North Carolina, by President Benjamin Harrison in the early 1890s. Obviously, as one of the leading bishops of a major black denomination and a loyal supporter of the Republican Party, he had captured the attention of the national Republicans. But he declined this "lucrative important position" because of his dedication to the church. In his stead, the bishop recommended the prominent layperson and newspaper editor John C. Dancy, who was confirmed undoubtedly because of Hood's support.[22] Hence, when given the test, Hood remained true to his convictions that the minister of the Gospel did not have sufficient time for political office. In 1913 Hood made several statements in his episcopal address to the Ninety-Seventh Annual Session of the New York Conference that illustrate his conception of his role: "I am not a politician, never was, never shall be. My special work is on religious lines. The work of building up the kingdom of our Lord and His Christ. But I am not insensible to the fact that the accomplishment of the best results in religious affairs will depend largely upon favorable conditions in civil affairs."[23]

As Christian leaders, ministers were believed to have a political role to play, but they must never allow themselves to become so wrapped up in political activities and ambitions for office that they would become politicians. Hood thought of himself in that light, and he sought to establish the same as a guiding rule for ministers under his charge during the many years he held the episcopal chair. But whatever he chose to call himself and however much he remained devoted primarily to the advancement of the church by carrying out his ecclesiastical responsibilities as a minister, Hood was, nonetheless, a politician who had an abiding interest in political affairs. His conception of the ministry, however, did

not permit him to imagine that a minister of the Gospel could possibly
have a calling to engage in civic and community work as a ministry in and
of itself. To him, as to most people of this era, ministry meant a collection
of duties *as a vocation* that was tied clearly, if not solely, to sacerdotal,
ritualistic, ecclesiastical affairs and institutions. A minister could be politically informed and had the responsibility of passing that information on
to his parishioners, but he could not be a politician and remain true to his
calling as a minister of the Gospel.

Hood advocated in strong terms for an educated ministry in the
church. In his address to the 1878 North Carolina Annual Conference, he
noted that an educated minister assisted the church in keeping abreast of
changing times. "An educated ministry is the demand of the present time.
A demand that must be met if we hope to keep pace with the times."[24] It
was necessary for ministers and parents to take full advantage of public or
"good common school" education. To attempt achieving a high school
training without building upon the elementary education would render
one more of a fool than a scholar and would be fatal in its effects. Of
course, this attitude was consistent with the attitude that existed throughout the leadership of all the denominations of the time. Both black and
white denominational leaders saw education as a significant level to raise
an oppressed race to a level of wealth and to demonstrate their capacity
for citizenship and leadership. If there were those who claimed that only
an understanding of the Bible was sufficient for the Christian minister,
Hood had an apt and piercing response, as noted by the recorder of the
1878 North Carolina Annual Conference proceedings. "Said he, if we
know the Bible, we would not, as preachers, need to know anything else;
but, we can't understand the Scriptures without knowing something else.
We must have an educated ministry."[25] With these words, Hood gave his
endorsement to the report from the conference's education committee.

Hood adopted a collaborative approach in his dealing with lay people
and ministers. He stated that the ministers themselves would succeed
best when they took similar approaches. In his episcopal address to the
Central North Carolina Conference meeting in Greensboro in 1899, the
bishop cataloged many successful ventures in building and reconstructing
churches throughout the annual conference. He noted activities in Durham, Franklinton, Marshville, Waymans, and Laurinburg. He attributed
some of the success to the willingness of the presiding elders to assist
local ministers in carrying out their duties. But a single sentence probably
best captures his philosophy: "Possibly, one reason for the wonderful
work done in this Conference is the complete harmony among Elders,
Pastors and people."[26]

In his episcopal address to the fifth assembly of the West Central

North Carolina Conference held in Monroe in November 1914, Hood spoke at greater length about the relationship between the minister and the congregation.[27] He insisted that ministers should not be "hirelings," individuals pursuing their work merely for salaries. Rather, their very hearts should be wrapped up in their ministerial duties. He also called upon ministers not to take an "independent" attitude toward the congregation. Presumably Hood referred to a detached relationship, one not characterized by personal involvement and mutual sharing. Indeed, Hood stated, the minister and the congregation should have a relationship of mutual dependence. The bishop also seemed to suggest that material return or wages were apt to be awarded more generously by the people if the pastor had demonstrated generosity and concern toward the congregation. "The idea of the Shepherd and the Flock is the one thing emphasized by the great Teacher. The Shepherd who gives the best service to the sheep, who takes the best care of them, who makes the greatest sacrifice for them, is the one [who] has the greatest benefit. He who disregards the interest of his sheep, will have the poorest sheep, and will receive the least return."[28]

The bishop also counseled the ministers that their example plays a great role in the quality of the spiritual life of the people. His position was that if the minister seeks to be independent of the people, they will develop an attitude of independence regarding the minister. If the minister adopts an attitude that "is selfish and narrow, and ill-natured," then the congregation could be expected to adopt the same posture. The best method for a minister's enhancing his or her own happiness is striving to put happiness into the lives of others. This principle also applies to the male minister's treatment of his wife. The minister should be respectful, loving, helpful, a provider of comforts. The quality of the marriage relationship also impacts the manner in which the minister is treated by the people. Hood warned ministers that the people watch intensely every "word or deed" of the minister, and a misstep could easily damage the spiritual program of the church. In sum, Hood stated, "In all things the minister should be the very best example of good behavior; of untiring energy and of unselfish devotion to his work."[29]

Hood was not one who merely exhorted and criticized. He also praised good, solid ministers who devoted their lives to their work. Throughout his writings and speeches there are references to ministers from various backgrounds, living and dead, who conducted their pastoral and ministerial work with honor and righteousness. For example, the bishop at the annual conference held in Tarboro, North Carolina, in 1880, commented on the life and contributions of David Hill, a young minister who in July 1864 journeyed south from New England under the missionary appointment of Bishop J. J. Clinton but contracted yellow fever soon after arriving in eastern North Carolina and died. Hood praised the self-educated minister as "a hard student" who had mastered several languages. God's will must be done, but Hood wondered, "What a power he might have been in Zion could he have been spared!"[30]

Hood congratulated black ministers not only for their tremendous contributions to building up the church but also for their contributions to the peace and well-being of society at large. By the time of the 1899 Central North Carolina Annual Conference, lynching and other violent acts against blacks were widespread, particularly in the South. Many black ministers spoke out forcefully and boldly against these atrocities. One notes in the recorded statements, comments, and addresses of these ministers that they often went to great pain to denounce crime, especially rape, while concomitantly denouncing, however moderately or forcefully, the vigilante act of lynching individuals accused of particular crimes.[31] They deplored the illegality and injustice of the death penalty without a fair trial and spoke in philosophical terms about how the disregard for the rights of the accused contributed in the long run to the breakdown of law and order across society. Perhaps these ministers were sensitive to charges being leveled against them that while they were denouncing lynching, they were giving aid and comfort to criminals.

In his episcopal address, Hood drew attention to the efforts of some white newspapers to blame African American ministers for these alleged crimes. In so doing he provided a sustained defense of black ministers based on their contribution to law and order in society.[32] He attempted to show that African American preachers, "especially those belonging to denominations with a central authority sufficiently strong to enforce obedience to discipline [for example, Zion Methodists themselves!] were among the most conservative and most useful citizens. So far from being responsible for the crimes of the degraded portion of the race, they were the very salt of the earth." "Whites had no idea," he argued, "how much was owing to the negro preachers for the good behavior of large numbers of our people or for the harmony that exists in most places between the races." Take away these ministers, he said, from "this mass of uncultured people,—over whom most of the white people make but little if any effort to exercise a moral or Christian influence—and pandemonium would reign." Those who committed crimes such as rape and murder, he noted, constituted a certain "class of Negroes" who were not touched by the influence of the black preacher or the church.[33]

One might fault Hood for apparently accepting so uncritically the premise that blacks were being lynched because they were suspected of having committed certain crimes. In reality, most persons lynched were political or economic leaders in the black community who thus constituted a threat to the white-controlled status quo. We could also question whether this emphasis upon the African American preacher's control over the behavior of the black community might not have been interpreted by many whites as a signal that rebellious behavior toward the status quo would be kept to a minimum by black ministers more interested in maintaining order and amicable relations between the races than the pursuit of economic and political justice and equity. But Hood's basic premise must not be overlooked by his harshest critics. He demanded of ministers the highest standards of deportment and believed that the standards they set had a considerable positive impact upon the black church, the African American community, and society in general.

These comments must not be taken to signify that the Zion ministers of Hood's day were mere pawns at the whim of episcopal officers and presiding elders. Individual members and groups often challenged even bishops, including James Hood, when they believed that their ministerial or personal rights were being imperiled or some aspect of Christian tradition or doctrine was being subverted or neglected. I have suggested above that black Methodist ministers had the option of realigning with competing groups as a means for personal or professional advancement or to exculpate themselves from unfavorable conditions. The documents of the time are replete with evidence that the bishops of the Zion connections were not all powerful, that they were subject to the General Conference, the assembly of ministers, and, eventually, some laity throughout the denomination. The editor or recorder of the 1888 General Conference proceedings noted that that General Assembly of Zionites had been "one of the most, if not the most memorable session of the AME Zion General Conference in the history of the Connection."[34] Perhaps one reason was that Bishop Hood was challenged on at least three occasions, despite the fact that the assembly was conferring in his home state and at the site of his earliest work in North Carolina, St. Peter's Church in New Bern.

The third day's session saw an action by Elder Alexander Walters that in and of itself would have made this conference memorable. This resolution said in brief that the General Conference should look into the matter of Bishop Hood's having endorsed the idea that slaveholders should have been compensated by the federal government for the people they held in bondage. (More precisely, Hood had argued that had slaveholders been compensated, they would not have regarded themselves as having been defrauded and would not have been taking out their resentment against blacks by perpetuating acts of oppression. Hood's primary concern was not the compensation of slaveholders per se but securing justice for blacks. Nevertheless, such an idea was anathema for the great majority of African Americans and racially progressive whites.) The original resolution was softened somewhat after a vigorous discussion. But it is clear that the entire assembly took the matter with utmost urgency, and Hood's episcopal robe did not in and of itself shield him from some possible censure, which never came.[35] In a subsequent session Hood was presented with an appeal arising from his episcopal district of New England dissenting from "his decision that the pastor is chairman of the Church meeting." He was requested to present that appeal to the Committee on Appeals, which it is assumed he did.[36]

On May 15, the twelfth day of the meeting, a tense exchange occurred between Walters and Hood. It is not altogether clear what the substance of Hood's remarks was meant to convey. At any rate, he did make "some conciliatory remarks to the Conference, stating that he was pleased to notice the development of a temper to reasonably consider important matters. He wanted the brethren to get out of the idea that the Board of Bishops was in antagonism with the views of the members of the Conference." Hood claimed that the board acted "to produce harmony in this body." Apparently, the General Conference had reached the conclusion that they should elect two new bishops, whereas Hood and the majority of the bishops felt that one would suffice. At some point the bishop must have made a remark about "young men." Elder Walters, who was one of the party that argued for an increased number of bishops, inquired if that remark should be taken to connote "antagonism." At that point Hood responded with a comment that could hardly be taken to indicate a desire for reconciliation. "Bishop Hood said the Bishops have been to young men as the man was to the bug on its back, turn it over, and said, 'go as any other bug.'" Perhaps Hood meant that he endeavored to treat younger ministers no differently than older ones. But the reference to "bug" appears to indicate some hostility or anger on Hood's part. Bishop Lomax, who was allied with Hood, spoke "in happy strains," according to the recorder, of his favor to the younger men, so much so that he was "considered to be partial to them."[37] This statement seems to represent Lomax's effort either to distance himself from Hood's comments or attitude or to smooth out a tense situation.

Hood and the Zion ministers were sometimes challenged at the annual conferences, where understandably they exercised greater power over individual ministers than at a connection-wide assembly in the General Conference, which involved ministers who were not under their immediate supervision and might very well be under the jurisdiction of a rival bishop. The Reverend J. H. Steward noted at the 1899 North Carolina Conference that despite his santification or attainment of Christian perfection, he had not been granted a pastoral appointment. Steward referred to a number of charges that had been made against him. He concluded his statements by claiming that Hood "did not have the feeling for him as he used to have." When a motion was made that, in being reconciled to the church once again, Steward had the confidence of the conference, Hood "arrested" the motion long enough to make a point. He "stated that he had nothing against Bro. Steward since he had informed him that he was in line with the church, but he was against any one that was against the interests of the Connection." The motion then passed.[28] The extent of the discord between Steward and the Conference is unclear; nor is it clear when he was assigned a pastorate. The point of this exchange is that individual ministers felt free even at the local level to challenge bishops under certain circumstances, and bishops felt obligated, morally and/or politically, to clarify their positions.

Sometimes the ministers demonstrated their dissatisfaction with the bishops through the pages of the official denominational organ, the *Star of Zion*. For example, there was a battle in the denomination from the 1880s until the end of the period under study between those who desired to increase the number of bishops and make other changes in the church and the more traditional Zionites, like Hood, who opposed some of these measures, including the election of a significantly greater number of bishops. A running line in Hood's argument was that the minister should not be an ambitious office seeker. He should wait to be asked to take a certain position. Buttressing his argument, Hood often pointed out that he was selected by others for the episcopacy and other church and political offices, that he did not seek the positions.

Edward Derusha Wilmot Jones (1871–1935) was one of the young men in Zion who crossed literary swords with the senior bishop. He was the son of Bishop S. T. W. Jones, who served as the sixteenth bishop of Zion from 1868 until his death in 1891, and Mary J. Jones, a pioneer in mission work in her own right. E. D. W. Jones, ordained an elder in 1891, became a member of the Western North Carolina Conference, although his roots were in Washington, D.C. He became the forty-first bishop of the AMEZ Church in 1924. Besides describing him as eloquent and charismatic in personality, Bishop Walls spoke of him as a gifted writer.[39] During a literary exchange between Jones and Hood in early 1904, Jones took issue with the perceived attempt to disregard the input of the younger members of Zion. Jones emphasized his conviction that Zion had always been a church for young people and that a person's youth should not exclude him from office. He directed the readers' attention to a number of influential leaders in the connection who themselves were strong forces in Zion when they were young, among them Bishop Hood. He also reminded Zion readers that both Bishop Hood and Lomax had pushed young men along the way, to their credit. The office of bishop, however lofty and holy, was not to be used to stifle the aspirations of the young, Jones argues.[40] This whole debate over the episcopacy and issues arising from it requires greater exploration. But it is obvious that Hood, despite his clear and pronounced viewpoints on the nature and role of the ministry, did not succeed in stifling debate among ministers under his immediate episcopal jurisdiction or elsewhere through the connection.

Hood, Religious "Skepticism," and Biblical Interpretation

Over the course of his career, Hood responded to a number of theological challenges. During the post–Civil War era of American religious history, significant intellectual ideas and theories challenged the traditional understanding of religion in general and Christianity in particular. Darwinian scientific findings and theories raised serious doubts about the traditional, literal interpretation of the biblical account of the origins and nature of the universe and humanity. The historical-critical study of Scripture (an approach that did not take the traditional claims made about the authorship of the Bible or even the contents of the canon itself at face value but subjected the text to literary, historical, and critical study) caused quite a furor in many religious bodies. Increasingly, American scholars and lay people were introduced to other religious traditions such as Buddhism and Hinduism; and finding that non-Christian and Jewish religions also displayed lofty moral and ethical principles, some Christians began to question the uniqueness of Christianity as the road to salvation. Other issues, concerns, and theories emanating from the developing fields of psychology, sociology, and the theology of the Social Gospel all combined with the above cited trends to occasion the division of the American Christiandom into three broad areas: religious conservatism or fundamentalism, religious liberalism and modernism, and a broad range of moderate perspectives such as evangelical or Christocentric liberalism.[41] Religious fundamentalism or conservatism sought to retain as much as possible the literal and traditional understanding of the Bible and Christian tradition; the other perspectives sought in some fundamental way to come to grips with information and insights provided by these new intellectual developments while not surrendering what was regarded as the essential core of biblical and traditional Christian truths.

While we must be extremely cautious in assigning labels to particular individuals, including those in the African American tradition, I believe it is appropriate to class Hood as a religious conservative in his response to these intellectual challenges to traditional Christian religion. This is not to say that he did not tackle many of the issues of the time; he did not ignore significant developments. But in responding to these challenges, the bishop employed his understanding of Methodism and Christianity and his American and African American episcopal experience in such a fashion that he was progressive on social concerns while being conservative theologically. It was during this era that the bifurcation developed between socially active Christianity on one hand and evangelicalism and fundamentalism on the other. Christians who continued to emphasize the role of faith in changing the social order, not merely individuals, leaned toward a more liberal, nontraditional manner of scriptural interpretation. Those who emphasized spiritual change in the individual rather than a stress on social reform emphasized a more conservative, fundamentalist perspective. Hood represented many of those black denominational leaders and the black church generally, who continued to embrace social activism as a corollary and mandate of evangelicalism and fundamentalism, just as some of them or their spiritual forbears had done vis-à-vis the struggle against slavery.[42] In other words, they read the Bible conservatively and literally, but their interpretations were in the tradition of liberation.

The bishop apparently made few if any direct references to the historical-critical study of the Bible and Christian traditions. We may infer from his many statements on the nature of the Bible and Christian doctrine, however, that his basic response consisted in rejecting the critical approach. Hood remained committed to the traditional doctrine that the Bible was the pure, inspired word of God, infallible throughout. His commentary on the New Testament book of Revelation, *The Plan of the Apocalypse*, reflects a literalistic understanding of the book characteristic of contemporary interpretations. The visions given the writer, John, in that book foretold events that would extend over centuries, including the conversion of the Roman Emperor Constantine, the rise of the Roman Catholic Church, the emergence of Islam, and the success of Protestantism. Hood did not accept the historical-critical understanding of the book as an attempt by an early Christian writer to assure his contemporaries that Christ would soon and dramatically intervene in human affairs, conquer the oppressive and brutal Roman Empire, and readily institute the visible Kingdom or Rule of God upon earth.[43]

In the apparent conflict between Charles Darwin's scientific theories on the evolution of the universe and humanity and the account believed to have been written by Moses under the direct inspiration of God, the traditionalists, including the bishop, rejected evolution of humanity for a literal interpretation of the Genesis account that suggested instantaneous and complete creation of the world and humanity within a week. Hood embraced this traditional understanding, not even attempting an allegorical interpretation that would offer some basis of consistency between the scientific theories and the biblical tradition, and he labeled as "skeptics" those who denied this and other traditional doctrines and interpretations.

Hood's eighth sermon in *The Christian Pulpit*, "Creation's First Born, Or The Earliest Gospel Symbol," is based upon the text of Genesis 1:3. Hood opened the sermon by claiming that the Genesis account was God's "own account of his own creation, written by the inspired pensman," whom he called "the inspired historian." It is very clear that Hood took issue with Darwinian science when he asserted that humanity's "best efforts" had been employed to derive a creation at variance with the biblical account. But such nonsense, as Hood would term it, as was propounded by these "infidel scientists" fell far short of the reasonable and inspired biblical account. Infidels had succeeded only in retrogressing in intellect since the days of the prophet Isaiah. Whereas the prophet condemned those who fashioned gods of *gold*, the modern person of God must take issue with the infidels who placed their trust in *protoplasm* (an obvious reference to the evolutionary theory that all life began as simple protoplasm). Hood asked, "Can that be considered a high order of intellect, which is willing to lose itself in a little speck of matter? which finds its creator in what can be handled by the creature?"[45] Any god created by modern humanity should at least represent a step beyond the infidelity of Isaiah's day. For those who would condemn the traditionalists for not using reason to understand the world, Hood not only attempted to point out the unreasonableness of Darwinian theories but also insisted that true reason is always in accordance with the revelation of God; any other type would be "unsanctified human reason," apt to lead one astray. Reflecting theological and philosophical arguments traditionally used to prove the existence of God, Hood insisted that a First Cause must necessarily exist and that until proven otherwise, that First Cause must be accepted as God.

Hood further insisted that the entire creation was only approximately six thousand years old. Everything that contemporary scientists and scholars reasonably knew, in Hood's view, constituted less than Adam, the first human, knew the first day of his existence. Indeed, much knowledge of astronomy could be traced back to the influence of the biblical records. Why put trust in unreliable human theories when humanity has the testimony of God? Those "infidel and [skeptical] philosophers" who attempted to deride the biblical account by pointing out that light existed before God created the sun and other luminous bodies demonstrate their ignorance. God "could as easily have created light independent of them as with" these liminaries. "[God] is not dependent upon any second cause; his resources are infinite; he doeth what he will in his own way, according to his own pleasure. He is the great fountain of light, and in him is no darkness, but light ineffable and eternal. He could not, therefore, give an exhibition of himself without producing light."[46] The bishop proceeded in his sermon by focusing upon the light of the Gospel. He spoke of the purity of the Gospel, how it retained its pristine quality in the face of "every foul system—heathenism, paganism, Mohammedanism [Islam]," and all "corrupting influences." Hood was later joined in this rejection of Darwinism by contemporaries such as the AME Jabez P. Campbell and the Episcopalian James T. Holly.[47]

It is necessary, however, to put Hood's bibically conservative interpretations into the larger context of the man and his time lest he be seen as a caricature. First, Hood's position must not be read as that of an unlearned and uninformed person. His writings reflect a wealth of knowledge and exposure to various ideas. For example, in some of his published articles, he demonstrated that, notwithstanding his opposition to evolutionary theories, he had a knowledge and appreciation of science. He indicated a sophisticated knowledge of astronomy, given the level of scientific knowledge at the time and the fact that he was not a scientist. Surprisingly (at least to this writer), Hood accepted the possibility that intelligent life comparable to human beings might exist in other worlds. In his sermon "Thy Kingdom Come," preached at the general conference of the Zion Church in May 1900, he stated explicitly that God's sovereignty extended over innumerable worlds of the universe: "Every twinkling star in the heavens is the sun of a solar system around which unnumbered planets [and] other satellites revolve. Many of these suns are vastly larger than ours, occupy much more room in space, and are naturally supposed to be surrounded by a larger number of satellites."[48]

Again, probably reflecting the state of astronomical knowledge of the time, Hood numbered eight planets in this solar system and made interesting comments concerning their revolutions and orbits through the heavens and their relation to earth. He referred specifically to "inhabitants" on Venus and Uranus and wished it were possible for him to visit Venus so that he might capture the view of Earth that they must experience. Furthermore, Hood noted the great fascination of astronomers fifty years earlier with the irregular revolutions of Uranus, some later postulating the existence of another planet.[49] Consistent with his faith in the sovereignty of God over the entire universe, the bishop posed the possibility that a Christlike figure had been sent to each of the other worlds in the universe. In an article on the incarnation of Christ, "Divine-Humanity," published just before Christmas 1903 in the *Star of Zion*, Hood began, "If other planets are inhabited with rational creatures, it is quite possible that they, like us, have needed a Saviour, and that one has been sent, and that they, like us, have rejoiced in the glorious gift."[50] Throughout, his writ-

ings, sermons, and speeches reflect the continual accumulation of knowledge from science, history, geography, religion, and other fields. While we
must note that many of his ideas, such as the possibility of inhabitants on
Venus, are dated, yet we also observe a creative and flexible mind. His
biblical conservatism did not reflect an ignorant mind.

A second point is that Hood, like many other religious leaders and
denominations, was attempting to defend the Bible and Christian tradition from what he envisioned as direct, atheistic assaults. What was at
stake was religious authority. Since its advent during the sixteenth-
century reformation in its break with Roman Catholicism, Protestantism
had claimed that the Bible was the chief source of religious authority,
reflecting the will of God. Many if not most Protestants in the United
States would claim that it was the sole authority. To deny one word of the
Bible as lacking precise, absolute, factual truth was perceived as laying
the entire sacred tradition open to human reasoning with varying interpretations and thus running the risk that the whole idea of God and the
sacred, revealed truth would collapse. Indeed, many persons propounding
evolutionary theories found little need for an active god's intervention and
participation in the world, and some were practically atheistic or agnostic,
including Charles Darwin himself. Whereas some religious leaders and
scholars sought to find a common ground of accommodation between science and traditional religion, others saw the matter in more traditional and
absolutist terms.

A third consideration forced its way upon blacks and racially progressive or tolerant whites of the era. For some time during the nineteenth
century, there were pseudoscientists who propounded polygenesis, the
concept that various races of humanity developed from different parents.[51]
Even when it did not embrace the notion of polygenesis, evolutionary
theory left open the possibility that a naturalistic, random development of
humanity had resulted in unequal development among the various
branches of humanity. In both schools of thought, the so-called natural,
genetic inferiority of blacks to whites received scholarly and scientific
sanction. Black Christians and the majority of white Christians refuted the
notion that all humanity was not descended from Adam and Eve. Black
Christians, much more consistently and passionately than their white
counterparts, went further and insisted that their common heritage,
backed by divine revelation, meant that all people were equal brothers
and sisters. Thus the Bible, not science as propounded by some whites,
was the chief foundation upon which blacks struggled to attain, maintain,
and expand their civil and other temporal rights and equities. The problem that some modern students of religion and the Bible have with "oppressive" elements in the Christian canon, especially regarding slavery,

must not be read back into the thinking of these religious leaders.[52] For these nineteenth- and early-twentieth-century denominational leaders, the entire Bible, not simply the prophetic tradition or the Synoptic Gospels, was a document of liberation from spiritual and temporal domination when correctly understood. For black and many white Christians, its pages guaranteed that all people were equal and that their God-given equality buttressed the demand for justice and equity in all aspects of society.

A fourth point, which is related to the preceding point, is that the biblical tradition, when interpreted literally, refuted the notion that African peoples had no substantial history. A tragic consequence of racism and white supremacy is that history is too often read solely from a Eurocentric perspective. The contributions, successes, and life stories of other people have not consistently received sufficient treatment. Black Christians during the period under study took the story of Ham and the genealogical tables in the Hebrew Bible or Christian Old Testament as authentication of black history and greatness. They wisely and accurately interpreted the so-called curse on Ham as in fact not a *divine* curse upon any one branch or the totality of the branches of Ham's descendants and especially not upon the ancestors of Africans on the continent or in the diaspora. Rather, these black Christians found assurance from the genealogical tables that the descendants of Ham, far from being a race of slaves, actually triumphed and figured gloriously, founding great empires and sharing in the ancestry of Jesus Christ. Not only were the Ethiopians and Egyptians claimed for the black race, but a literal interpretation of these genealogical tables also placed the Babylonians and Assyrians in this category.

Hood, accepting the Bible as divinely inspired, interpreting it literally, and being versed in the works of other black scholars on the antiquity of the black race, shared in the conviction of its greatness and former glory. An arresting article in the *Star of Zion,* November 16, 1893, points out Hood's interest in this matter. In this article the bishop reviewed several books that had appeared in that year: a collection of three sermons by the Reverend G. L. Blackwell; collection of poetry composed by Zion clergy and laity and edited by the Reverend B. F. Wheeler; a collection of sacred songs, some of black composition, compiled by W. H. Sherwood; and Rufus L. Perry's *The Cushite,* which dealt with the early history of African peoples. Hood commented quite favorably on each of these works but reserved his highest praise and elation for Perry's book. *The Cushite* so engrossed him that he read some 175 pages in the first sitting. He wished to write a more extended review than the three paragraphs that he devoted to Perry's book, which was about three times what he wrote on the other books he reviewed. But in the space he had, he noted that the book exhibited "profound learning, deep, long and painstaking record'; pre-

dicted that it would become "a standard" on the subject matter; and rejoiced that Perry had used his intellectual skills to present an account
genuinely reflective of African achievement. "Dr. Perry's classical knowledge has enabled him to read the only histories in their original tongue,
not warped by the prejudices of Caucasian writers," Hood said. "This fact
adds greatly to the value of the book." Hood suggested that all people,
especially African Americans, should digest the contents of Perry's work
"respecting the ancient greatness of the descendants of Ham, the ancestors of the American Negro."[53]

Some modern scholars, like many in the past, might ridicule, overlook, or contest this interpretation of ancient history. Many may character-
ize it as too sweeping. One thing is certain, however. This interpretation
of the biblical record pointed to a position that in the last decades of
the twentieth century is becoming much more acceptable, even in white
academic circles: that the black race was an active and even a crucial participant in the ancient affairs of northern Africa and other areas of the
Middle East or Afro-Asiatic world.[54] Despite intermittent periods of political and economic progress, black Americans as a whole during the nineteenth and early twentieth centuries faced a host of oppressive and
proscriptive conditions, including enslavement, racial segregation, disfranchisement, and acts of terrorism. In the face of these and other adversities,
and additionally burdened with the reality that black history was given
insufficient attention by most scholars, black religious leaders and other
learned blacks like James W. Hood turned to the Bible and secured from it
a more complete and benevolent portrayal of black history and humanity.
However much we might critique a literalistic reliance on Scripture as
reflective of precise historical details, the Bible, understood as the pure
word of God by black traditionalists, played a crucial role during a time
when there were too few professionally trained African American scholars.
We might also take note that religiously traditionalist African Americans
were not alone in employing Scripture as a reservoir of accurate history.

Conclusion

The preceding pages certainly do not present an exhaustive theological portrait of the dynamic and creative individual James W. Hood. Nevertheless, this chapter has alerted the reader to the significance of the
southern leader in both ecclesiastical and political circles. As we specifically examined Hood's views regarding the church and ministry, it is apparent that he held a traditionalist understanding of the church but with
a racial "twist" or application of that understanding for the African American experience. The church in Hood's views was not simply important

as a means of bringing spiritual redemption, but the black church was a providential lever by which God was acting in history to uplift the black race. While ministers must place first priority on the work of the church, at certain points in history, such as the Civil War and Reconstruction years, they may be called upon to represent the race in political affairs. Even when they were not political officeholders, they still had the responsibility of being informed regarding civic matters and advising their flocks accordingly. One must not forget, furthermore, that Hood believed that simply spreading Christianity gave people moral power to face debilitating circumstances and strive for freedom and equity. For Hood the Bible was a document of liberation, when correctly understood. His traditionalist or conservative understanding of the Bible did not hinder his intellectual curiosity and creativity. Finally, Hood represented the mainstream black denominational leader in the South during the 1860–1920 period. A case study of Hood contributes immensely to our comprehension of how these southern black leaders were laboring for both God and race.

Notes

This article resulted in large part from Senior Faculty and Humanities Center grants awarded by the University of Georgia.

1. See the *African Methodist Episcopal Zion Quarterly Review* 8 (Nos. 1 and 2, 1899): 1–9. Some of the early *AMEZ Quarterly Review* issues are not clearly marked regarding the exact months or volumes. Where this information is lacking, I have attempted to approximate the volume number by comparing known publication dates of other issues. I have also simply included information such as "Nos. 1 and 2" if more exact information has not been provided. Also see Hood's "The Character and the Persuasive power of the Christian Religion," *Quarterly Review* 13 (January–March 1904): 11–19.
2. *Quarterly Review* 13 (January–March 1904): 18, 17.
3. See Hood's *Sketch of the Early History of the AMEZ Church*, 59–66.
4. Ibid., 60.
5. Ibid., 62.
6. *AMEZ Quarterly Review* 8 (April 1899): 6–7.
7. Hood, *Sketch*, 62.
8. Ibid., 63.
9. Ibid., 65.
10. Ibid., 65–66.
11. Minutes, North Carolina Annual Conference, 1876, 7–8. Minutes, Central North Carolina Conference, 1882, 11–12.
12. Minutes, Central North Carolina Conference, 1882, 11–12.

13. Minutes, North Carolina Annual Conference, 1899, 24.
14. For the account of Williams's readmission to the conference, see Minutes, Central North Carolina Annual Conference, 1881, 7–8.
15. Ibid., 8.
16. Minutes, North Carolina Annual Conference of AMEZ Church, 1876, 8. The entirety of the preceding discussion is found on 7–8.
17. Minutes, Central North Carolina Conference, 1881, 9, 10–11.
18. *Star of Zion*, November 14, 1884, 1.
19. Ibid.
20. Hood, *One Hundred Years*, 19.
21. Ibid. Quote is taken from 19. Also, see 18–19 for discussion.
22. Minutes, New England Annual Conference, 1891, 36.
23. Minutes, New York Annual Conference, 1913, 25.
24. Minutes, North Carolina Annual Conference, 1878, 4.
25. Ibid., 18.
26. Minutes, Central North Carolina Conference, 1899, 76–78 for entire discussion; 78 for quote.
27. Minutes, West Central North Carolina Conference, 1914, 3–9 for entire episcopal address; 3–4 for discussion on the relationship between ministers and the people.
28. Ibid., 3.
29. Ibid., 4.
30. Minutes, North Carolina Annual Conference, 1880, 8.
31. Baptist as well as Methodist black ministers expressed their concern on these issues. See, e.g., Elias C. Morris, "1899 Presidential Address to the National Baptist Convention," in Milton C. Sernett, ed., *Afro-American Religious History: A Documentary Witness* (Durham: Duke University Press, 1985), 272–84, but especially 276–77.
32. Minutes, Central North Carolina Conference, 1899, especially 85–87.
33. Ibid., 86.
34. Minutes, General Conference of the AMEZ Church, 1888, 77.
35. Ibid., 18–19; Hood's Episcopal Address, Minutes, New York Annual Conference, 1888, 6–12.
36. Ibid., 43.
37. Ibid., 57–58.
38. Minutes, North Carolina Annual Conference, 1899, 24–25.
39. William Walls, *The African Methodist Episcopal Zion Church: Reality of the Black Church* (Charlotte, N.C.: A.M.E. Zion Pub. House, 1974), 598–99.
40. *Star of Zion*, March 24, 1904, 1.
41. For some excellent surveys and insights on the intellectual challenges facing historic and traditional Christianity during the period 1860–1920, see, e.g., Robert T. Handy, ed., *Religion in the American Experience: The Pluralistic Style* (New York: Harper & Row, 1972), 116–29; Handy et al., eds., *American Christianity: An Historical Interpretation with Representative Documents, Volume II, 1820–1960* (New York: Charles Scribner's Sons, 1963), 213–416; Sydney E.

Ahlstrom, *A Religious History of the American People* (New Haven: Yale University Press, 1972), 731–872; and Winthrop S. Hudson and John Corrigan, *Religion in America: An Historical Account of the Development of American Religious Life*, 5th ed. (New York: Macmillan, 1992), 203–311.

42. The connection between evangelical Christianity and the quest for social progress is illustrated in David O. Moberg, *The Great Reversal: Evangelism versus Social Concern* (Philadelphia: Lippincott, 1972). Ronald C. White Jr., *Liberty and Justice for All: Racial Reform and the Social Gospel (1877–1925)*, The Rauschenbusch Lectures, N.S. 2 (New York: Harper & Row, 1990), masterfully points out the connection between racial reform and the Social Gospel Movement. White lays to rest a common but inaccurate assumption that leaders of the Social Gospel did not address issues of race. He also points out that the Social Gospel Movement was supported by both whites and blacks. Peter J. Paris, a social ethicist, has laid a firm foundation for further historical exploration of social teachings in the major black denominations since the Civil War. See his *The Social Teaching of the Black Churches* (Philadelphia: Fortress Press, 1985). For an overall analysis of the Social Gospel Movement, see Donald K. Gorrell, *The Age of Social Responsibility: The Social Gospel in the Progressive Era, 1900–1920* (Macon, Ga.: Mercer University Press, 1988). Although most of the above cited works do not focus upon fundamentalism or evangelicalism, they all amply demonstrate that evangelical ministers and laity were involved in the efforts to reform society.

43. James W. Hood, *The Plan of the Apocalypse* (York, Pa.: P. Anstadt & Sons, 1900).

44. Hood, *Pulpit*, 105–121. James W. Hood, *The Negro in the Christian Pulpit* (Raleigh, N.C.: Broughton, 1884), 105–21.

45. Ibid., 105.

46. Ibid., 110.

47. Ibid., 115; Moses Nathaniel Moore, "Orishatukeh Faduma and the New Theology," *Church History* 63 (March 1994); 60–80, especially 65.

48. *Daily Star of Zion* (Washington, D.C.), May 2 and 3, 1900, 1-3; the quote is taken from 2. The remainder of the sermon was published in the May 4, 1900, publication of this newspaper.

49. Ibid., 2.

50. *Star of Zion*, December 24, 1903, 1.

51. For a historical analysis of white attitudes toward the personhood of blacks, see George M. Frederickson, *The Black Image in the White Mind: the Debate on Afro-American Character and Destiny, 1817–1914* (New York: Harper & Row, 1971). The following chapters are of particular relevance to this discussion: chapter 3, "Science, Polygenesis, and the Proslavery Argument," 71–96; chapter 8, "The Vanishing Negro: Darwinism and the Conflict of the Races," 228–55; chapter 9, "The Negro as Beast: Southern Negrophobia at the Turn of the Century," 256–82.

52. During the 1980s if not before, professionally trained black scholars of the Bible began ongoing critical assessments of biblical interpretation as it related to African American life. See, e.g., Cain Hope Felder, *Troubling Biblical Waters:*

Race, Class, and Family, Bishop Henry McNeal Turner Studies in North American Black Religion, Vol. III (Maryknoll, N.Y.: Orbis Books, 1989); and Felder, ed., *Stony the Road We Trod: African American Biblical Interpretation* (Minneapolis: Fortress Press, 1991). These are indispensable, groundbreaking texts that represent scholarly activities among African American scholars to make the Christian canon and its interpretation more relevant to the liberation struggles of peoples of color, women, and the poor. I would caution these dedicated scholars, however, not to read the contemporary difficulties they find with the biblical texts back into the thinking of black denominational leaders and church people during the era of James W. Hood. As difficult as it might be for many of us to grasp during the last decade of the twentieth century, these earlier church people understood the Bible as God's pure—*and liberating*—word.

53. *Star of Zion*, November 16, 1893, 2.

54. A rather conservative or restrained representation of blacks in the ancient world is given in Frank M. Snowden Jr., *Blacks in Antiquity: Ethiopians in the Greco-Roman Experience* (Cambridge, Mass.: Belknap Press of Harvard University Press, 1970). Martin Bernal does not make the question of race a central concern in volume 1 of his *Black Athena*. But he does make it clear that he views the ancient Egyptian civilization as fundamentally black or Negroid. Given the fact that he portrays Egypt as the source for much of ancient Greek civilization, this is quite a statement. See his *Black Athena: The Afroasiatic Roots of Classical Civilization, Volume 1, The Fabrication of Ancient Greece 1785–1985* (New Brunswick, N.J.: Rutgers University Press, 1987). In the first volume Bernal finds himself largely in agreement with many black scholars of the ancient world. These scholars much more pointedly insist that ancient Egypt and Ethiopia were black civilizations and were the foundations for Greek and subsequent western civilizations. See, e.g., John G. Jackson, *Introduction to African Civilizations* (Secaucus, N.J.: Citadel Press, 1970); and Cheikh Anta Diop, *The African Origin of Civilization: Myth or Reality* (New York: Lawrence Hill, 1974).

Epilogue

The contents of this volume are offered as a contribution to the knowledge and understanding of African American religious life, an important goal in itself. However, there is good reason to note that this country's majority European American population in particular would profit from gaining a better understanding and consequent appreciation of this subject. Such an assertion is obviously made because of the tortured relationships of blacks and whites in the United States. Racism continues to be the most challenging domestic issue facing our people.

As a European American contributing to this work, I believe the most significant point I can make is to stress the challenge as well as the opportunity for whites not only to learn about but also to experience something of the depths of African American religious life, shaped as it has been by the oppressive history of slavery and discrimination. While African American readers will certainly profit from a careful consideration of this volume, its contents pose a particular invitation to European Americans to apprehend the identity and promise of the black community on a profound level.

An important part of such an experience is to recognize the central role of religious life and conviction among black people. The title of this volume, drawn from a line in one of the slave spirituals, expresses it eloquently—"Ain't Gonna Lay My 'Ligion Down." Religion *is* life and meaning, a bulwark in helping its adherents face an oppressive world. It expresses in remarkable ways both the suffering and the joy of the black experience, the indomitable spirit of a people whose religious anchor in the saving grace of Jesus will not let them go. The character of African American culture, marked as it is by many forms of oppression, has enabled this community to plumb the depths of the rich redemptive motifs of the Christian message in a truly remarkable way. At the same time, as this volume demonstrates, this Christian expression is shaped and influenced by a spirituality and religious heritage far removed from Christian hegemony.

The erosions of secularism have certainly affected African American life, but the "soul of black folks" is still most effectively communicated in religious tones, indelibly marked by their unique historical experience and the heritage of their African ancestors. Paul Tillich's thesis that religion is the substance of culture and culture the form of religion is amply demonstrated here. Several essays in this volume have also noted the intimate connection of religious life with a variety of aesthetic expressions; the worshiping community has provided the setting for music, oratory, poetry, and dance. In this setting we see some of the most creative demonstrations of African American culture.

A historical work of this kind could be characterized as an effort at conservation, or lifting up dimensions of a rich heritage not sufficiently explored. It is important to conserve because the subject material is so intimate to African American identity. Indeed, the conservative character of black people can be located at this point, where the values of the religious tradition are identified with the stability and strength of the black family. This fact is often lost to white consciousness in this country, which tends to identify blacks exclusively with liberal if not radical politics. To be sure, the conservatism of the black religious community is far removed from the conservatism of many white evangelicals as expressed today in the religious right. It is, rather, a religious and cultural conservatism that avoids extreme ideological expressions. Unlike the religious conservatism of many white denominations in the South, often fearful and belligerent toward those with whom they disagree, black religious conservatism is both more open and more generally focused on issues of discipleship than on divisive questions of theology.

The regional focus of this work was mentioned in the introduction, but it bears noting that many distinctions between the white population in South and North are decidedly more pronounced than is the case in the black population. This is understandable, given the history of the white communities in each region and the fact that most blacks in the North have their roots in the South. With regard to religious life, however, the distinction is pertinent for both black and white communities: the impact of the church and religious sentiments generally remain more conspicuous in the South. With the growing urbanization of the South, the black community in that region will have to become more intentional about cultivating its religious roots and celebrating its distinctive religious heritage.

Understandably, African Americans have never fully assimilated into the majority culture. Yet their religious life has exerted its impact upon that culture, bringing a unique gift of experiential religion conveyed in rhythmic bodily action and exuberant song. That gift is one we are called to share and to celebrate, letting it enhance and season the traditions that each of our religious communities brings to the nation's religious and cultural life. I hope this volume will make its own unique contribution in helping that to happen as well as deepening our understanding of the historical background that has given the peculiar shape and character to African American expressions of Christian faith and life.

—Paul Jersild

Contributors

Stephen W. Angell is Associate Professor of Religion at Florida A & M University in Tallahassee.

Jacqueline D. Carr-Hamilton is Assistant Professor in the Department of Religion at Virginia Polytechnic Institute and State University, Blacksburg.

Paul Jersild is Professor of Theology and Ethics at Lutheran Theological Southern Seminary in Columbia, South Carolina.

Alonzo Johnson is Assistant Professor in the Department of Religious Studies at the University of South Carolina, Columbia.

William Courtland Johnson is a Ph.D. candidate in the Department of History at the University of California–Riverside.

Sandy Dwayne Martin is Associate Professor in the Department of Religion at the University of Georgia, Athens.

Jon Michael Spencer is the Tyler and Alice Haynes Professor of American Studies and Professor of Music at the University of Richmond.

32
33